GOD'S ETERNAL PURPOSES FOR MANKIND

GOD'S ETERNAL PURPOSES FOR MANKIND

JAMES V. ROBERTSON, BS, THM, DD

CITI OF BOOKS

CITIOFBOOKS, INC.
3736 Eubank NE Suite A1
Albuquerque, NM 87111-3579
www.citiofbooks.com
Hotline: 1 (877) 389-2759
Fax: 1 (505) 930-7244

Ordering Information:

Quantity sales. Special discounts are available on quantity purchases by corporations, associations, and others. For details, contact the publisher at the address above.

Printed in the United States of America.

ISBN-13:   Softcover   979-8-89391-582-2

                  eBook   979-8-89391-583-9

Library of Congress Control Number: 2025905552

TABLE OF CONTENTS

ACKNOWLEDGMENTS

I first wish to publicly thank my Lord and Savior Jesus Christ for delivering me from the bondage of sin and Satan and for calling me unto His glory and virtue. Next, I wish to acknowledge and thank a special group of people who have surrounded me with their love and support through many situations, my late mother, Juliana D. Robertson; my brothers, Fitz F. Robertson and Charles H. Robertson; my sister, Angele P. Fraser, my daughters, Lois O. Robertson and Abigale S. O. Robertson; and my current pastors, Pastors David and Allyson Mendez of the Rochdale Shepherd House Open Bible Church, Queens, New York. I wish also to thank my cousin Rosalyne Gardiner for gracefully accepting the tedious task of proofreading this project.

I also wish to acknowledge and thank my teachers from the Community Bible Institute and Seminary, Brooklyn, New York—Professors Dr. Robert S. Thomas Sr., Dr. Beverly Jones, and the late Dr. Clarence Harris—for their labor of love in the ministry to equip and prepare me to honor the call of God on my life.

I dedicate this work to the loving memory of my mother, Juliana D. Robertson.

INTRODUCTION

One of the most thought-provoking and life-transforming themes we have experienced in the twenty-first century is that of purpose. *Purpose* is defined as the reason why something was done, created, or exists. Rick Warren, author of the books *The Purpose Driven Church* and *The Purpose Driven Life*, began a discussion on this theme that has captivated the hearts of theologians, ministers of the Gospel, and saints alike. The book *The Purpose Driven Church* topped the *Wall Street Journal* bestseller charts as well as the *Publishers Weekly* charts. *The Purpose Driven Life* was also on the *New York Times* bestseller list for over ninety weeks. It had sold over eighteen million copies by 2008 and thirty-two million copies by 2012. According to both the author and publisher, Simon & Schuster, fifty million copies were sold in more than eighty-five languages by 2020. A May 2005 survey of American pastors and ministers conducted by George Barna asked Christian leaders to identify what books were the most influential on their lives and ministries. *The Purpose Driven Life* was the most frequent response. The *Purpose Driven Church*, written prior to *The Purpose Driven Life*, was the second most frequent response (Wikipedia. org).

The late Dr. Myles Munroe made very tangible contributions to and expanded this discussion through his books *Purpose for Living, Understanding the Purpose and Power of Women, Purpose and Power of God's Glory, God's Purpose for Family and Marriage, The Purpose and Power of Praise, In Pursuit of Purpose, Purpose and Power of Authority, Understanding the Purpose and Power of Men, Understanding the Purpose and Power of Prayer,* and *Understanding the Purpose and Power of the Holy*

Spirit. The impact of the life and ministry of this gifted author, lecturer, teacher, pastor, business and government consultant, leadership and life mentor, and motivational speaker cannot be fully gauged by the awards and honors and OBEs (honorary doctorate degrees) he received.

In this presentation, I will seek to outline the purposes for which the Living God our Creator made mankind. God created man with the faculty of volition, which allows every person to choose their lifestyle and destiny. God has no delight in the death of the wicked. "Have I any pleasure at all that the wicked should die? Saith the Lord God, and not that he should return from his ways and live?" (Ezek. 18:23). "For God sent not His Son into the world to condemn the world, but that the world through Him might be saved" (John 3:17).

This work will provide everyone—scholars, believers, and unbelievers—an opportunity to grasp in clear terms the eternal purposes of God for the race of man. Aspects of my presentation that most assuredly will garner attention are the nature of angels and the constitution of man.

James V. Robertson
Queens, New York
May 1, 2023

CHAPTER 1

THE SPHERE OF GOD PRIOR TO HIS CREATION OF MAN

Since I will be using the King James Version of the Holy Bible as my primary reference for this thesis, I wish to enunciate evidence for the inspiration of this divine book. One of the miraculous pieces of evidence of the divine inspiration of the Bible is its unity. This annual bestseller comprises sixty-six books written over a period of 1,600 years (from 1500 BC to AD 100) by some forty people from different parts of the world, yet it is without contradiction. The unity of the scriptures is manifested in seven aspects as follows:[1]

a. The revelation or self-disclosure of God provided in the Old Testament by His names and works was expanded in the New Testament with the revelation of the Trinity, the relations of the Divine Persons, their relations to the race of man, and God's plan of redemption as expounded by Christ Himself on the Emmaus Road (Luke 24:27).

b. The fulfillment of prophecy—every instance of fulfilled prophecy is evidence of the accuracy, consistency, and progression of the scriptures and God's purposes.

---

1   Arthur W. Pink, *The Divine Inspiration of the Bible*, 31–33.

c. The union between the types and antitypes—most of the major truths in the New Testament were foreshadowed in the Old Testament.

d. The revelation of Satan and evil—this truth is expanded in the New Testament by the revelation of God's plan of redemption through the atoning work of Jesus Christ.

e. The doctrine of man and sin—the scriptures' record of man's failures is consistent in every dispensation.

f. The requirement of holiness in saints' conduct—the requirement of a holy lifestyle on the part of believers is consistent in every dispensation.

g. The continuity of purpose in the program of God—although the characteristic of each dispensation is unique, the divine purpose is one ending in an astounding consummation prophesied by God in the beginning.

I endorse the views of Tony Evans, who said, "God doesn't use His omniscience to win contests. He doesn't play Jeopardy or spin the Wheel of Fortune. Everything God knows is plugged into His eternal purposes."[2] Prior to the creation of the era of time (Gen. 1:1), God created Paradise, His dwelling place and the innumerable multitude of angels. God the Father's fellowship at that time was with His Son the Word (Rev. 19:13), the Holy Spirit, and the angels, in particular, the archangels. I will delve deeper into the nature of God's relationship with the angels in chapter 2 and will address the nature of God because it provides insight into His dealings with His creation.

Definition and Names of God

God is Deity, the Creator of the universe and source of all things, animate, inanimate, and spiritual, whether they be visible, invisible, thrones, dominions, principalities, or powers (Col. 1:16; John 1:1–3). I will now share the Creator/Elohistic names of God,[3] which provide some insight into His provision, protection, and involvement in the daily lives of those that trust in Him.

---

2   Tony Evans, *Our God Is Awesome*, 134.
3   Timothy Paul Jones, *Rose Book of Bible Charts, Maps and Timelines*, 36.

Adonai. "The Lord my Great Lord," God is the Master and majestic Lord (Ps. 8; Ezek. 16:8; Isa. 40:3–5).

El. The Strong One, He is more powerful than all false gods, He is dependable and will always overcome; the lad David's victory over the giant Goliath is tangible evidence of this truth (1 Sam. 17:49–51; Exod. 15:2; Num. 23:22; Deut. 7:9).

El Elohe Yisrael. God, the God of Israel, Israel's God is separate from all false gods of the world; Elijah's defeat of the eight hundred prophets of Baal, when fire from the Lord consumed the burnt offering set up in the midst of water, is tangible evidence of this truth (1 Kings 18:37–40; Gen. 33:20; Exod. 5:1; Ps. 106:48). *El Elyon.* The God Most High, He is the Sovereign God in whom we can trust. He has supremacy over all false gods; the worship and destruction of Dagon before the Ark of the Covenant is tangible evidence of this truth (1 Sam. 5:2–4; Gen. 14:17–22; Ps. 78:35; Dan. 4:34).

Elohim. The All-Powerful One Creator, He is the AllPowerful Creator of the universe. God knows all, creates all, and is everywhere; the Lord's confrontation with Job outlines this truth (Job 38:1–41; Gen. 1:1–3; Deut. 10:17; Ps. 68:1–35).

El Olam. The Eternal God, the Everlasting God, He is the Beginning and the End, the One who works His purposes throughout the ages. He gives strength to the weary; the testimony of the Lord God affirms this truth, "Fear not; I am the first and the last: I am He that is alive and was dead; and behold I am alive for evermore, Amen and have the keys of hell and of death" (Rev. 1:17b–18; Gen. 21:33; Ps. 90:1–2; Isa. 40:28).

El Roi. "The God who sees me." There are no circumstances in our lives that escape His fatherly awareness and care. God knows all our troubles; the confession of King David, "My substance was not hid from thee when I was made in secret and curiously wrought in the lowest parts of the earth. Thine eyes did see my substance yet being unperfect and in thy book all my members written, which in continuance were fashioned, when as yet there was none of them" (Ps. 139:15–16), affirms this truth (Gen. 16:11–14; Ps. 139:7–12).

El Shaddai. The All-Sufficient One, the God of the Mountains, God Almighty. He is the All-Sufficient Source of all our blessings. God is all-powerful; our problems are not too much for Him to handle; the Lord's deliverance of Israel from the Egyptian bondage is evidence of this truth (Exod. 14:26–31; Gen. 17:1–3; Ps. 90:2; Gen. 48:3; 49:25).

Immanuel. God with us, Jesus is God in our midst. In Him dwells all the fullness of the Deity; the Lord's address to the nation of Israel at Mount Sinai affirmed this truth (Exod. 19:3–6; Isa. 7:14: Matt. 1:23; Isa. 8:8–10).

I will now examine the redemptive names of God,[4] which addresses His faithfulness to His promises and His boundless and unchanging love and grace.

Jehovah, Jah, Yah. "I Am," "the One who is," "the Self-Existent One." God never changes; His promises never fail. When we are faithless, He remains faithful; the Lord's deliverance of Lot and his family is tangible evidence of this truth (Gen. 19:12–17; Exod. 3:14; 34:5–7; Ps. 102).

Jehovah-Jireh. The Lord will provide. As He provided a ram for Isaac, He provided His Son Jesus as the ultimate sacrifice for our sins. He will meet all our needs (Gen. 22:13–14; Ps. 23; Mark 10:45).

Jehovah-Mekaddishkem. The Lord who sanctifies. God sets us apart as a chosen people, a royal priesthood holy unto God, a people of His own. He cleanses our sin and helps us mature (Exod. 31:12–13; 1 Peter 1:15–16; 1 Thess. 5:23–24).

Jehovah-Nissi. The Lord is my banner. God gives us victory over the flesh, world, and the devil. Our battles are His, light against darkness and good against evil (Exod. 17:15–16; Deut. 20:3–4; Isa. 11:10–12).

Jehovah-Rapha. The Lord who heals. God has provided the final cure for spiritual, physical, and emotional sickness in Jesus Christ (Exod. 15:25–27; Ps. 103:3; 147:3).

Jehovah-Rohi. The Lord is my Shepherd. The Lord protects, provides, directs, leads, and cares for His people. God tenderly takes care of us as a strong and patient shepherd (Ps. 23:1–3; Isa. 53:6; Heb. 13:20).

---

4   Ibid., 36.

Jehovah-Sabaoth. The Lord of Hosts, the Lord of Armies. The Lord of the hosts of heaven will always fulfill His purposes even when the hosts of His earthly people fail; the Lord's deliverance of Israel against the armies of the Midianites and the Amalekites with Gideon and three hundred soldiers is tangible evidence of this truth (Judg. 8:28; 1 Sam. 1:3; 17:45; Ps. 46:7).

Jehovah-Shalom. The Lord is Peace. God defeats our enemies to bring us peace. Jesus is our Prince of Peace; He brings inner peace and harmony (Num. 6:22–27; Judg. 6:22–24; Heb. 13:20).

Jehovah-Shammah. The Lord is there, the Lord my Companion. God's presence is not limited to or contained in the tabernacle but is accessible to all who love and obey Him; the Lord's presence with and favor on Joseph in Egypt is tangible evidence of this truth (Gen. 41:38–45; Ezek. 48:35; Ps. 46).

Jehovah-Tsidkenu. The Lord our righteousness. Jesus is the King who comes from David's line and imparts His righteousness to us; the Lord's call and favor on Cornelius and his household is tangible evidence of this truth (Acts 10:1–45; Jer. 23:5–6; 33:16; Ezck. 36:26–27).

Nature of God: Essence and Attributes

Essence of God

By His self-disclosure in the scriptures, God provided man much information that permits persons to discern characteristics of His nature that are distinct from His works and roles as Creator, Guide, and Preserver. These qualities are shared by every member of the Godhead— Father, Son, and Holy Spirit. Four characteristics are evident in God's essence: spirituality, self-existence, immensity, and eternity.[5]

Spirituality. God is a spirit. He is not a material or corporeal substance, but a substance nonetheless (John 4:24). Other aspects of God's spirituality are that He is alive, He is invisible, and He is a person. He is a spirit that cannot be contained in a body; the Bible clearly states that Jesus was God manifested in the flesh according to

---

5   Henry Thiessen, *Lectures in Systematic Theology*, 2nd ed., 75.

the divine plan of God the Father to provide man's redemption. The scriptures referring to the kenosis says,

Being in the form of God... He made himself of no reputation and took upon Him the form of a servant and was made in the likeness of men. (Phil. 2:6–7)

In the beginning was the Word and the Word was with God and the Word was God...And the Word was made flesh and dwelt among us, and we beheld His Glory, the glory as of the only begotten of the Father, full of grace and truth. (John 1:1, 14)

Noteworthy is the fact that Jesus is only a part of and not the entire Godhead; hence, His being in the form of a body does not contradict God's incorporate reality.

Because God, unlike the dead gods of the heathen, is a living spirit, He is referred to often in scripture as the Living God (Josh. 3:10; 1 Tim. 3:15). The life of God is that eternal source that sustains all forms of life in the universe. It also refers to the fact that God possesses all the senses man enjoys and more; He sees, hears, and exercises the power of activity. He answered the prophet Elijah's prayer by consuming the sacrifice on the altar with fire from heaven (1 Kings 18:37–39; Ps. 115:3–8). God is also a person; He has a personality, an intellect, and emotions. He loves the world and hates sin; He is a jealous God. He exercises self-consciousness and self-determination (Eph. 1:9; Heb. 6:17).

Self-existence. God always existed; His existence is uncaused. There was never a beginning to His existence. Mankind and the universe were caused or created by Him; He is their source and sustenance. Accordingly, their source is external, but God has no source. He is the absolute infinity (Isa. 40:12–31).

Where were you when I laid the foundations of the earth? Declare if you have understanding. (Job 38:4)

Immensity. God created and sustains space. Without Him, there is no space; hence, He is, in no way, limited by space. He is above and beyond all space in the universe; God is both immanent and transcendent. His presence is everywhere in His fullness at the same time (Acts 17:24–28). "But will God indeed dwell on the earth? Behold the heaven and heaven of heavens cannot contain thee; how much less this house that I have built" (1 Kings 8:27). These were the words of King Solomon in the dedication of the temple in Jerusalem.

Eternity. Time, like space, was created by God and is sustained by Him; He exists outside of and beyond the boundaries of time. God exists by reason of His nature, which is not just life but eternal life. He always was and forever shall be God (Isa. 57:15). As Moses said, "From everlasting to everlasting, Thou art God" (Ps. 90:2).

Attributes of God

The attributes of God are grouped into two categories, natural and moral. Attributes are those characteristics of the Godhead that not only permit us to describe and distinguish Him but are evident in His relations with the universe. These qualities are objectively genuine features of God and not man's subjective conception. Theologians devised several classifications of the attributes of God. Dr. Henry Thiessen recorded the four most popular classifications. These are the natural and moral attributes, immanent and transitive attributes, positive and negative attributes, and lastly, the tripartite approach, which groups the attributes based on their association with the essence, intellect, and will of God.[6] I will use the natural and moral classifications for this presentation.

Natural attributes. These are the qualities of God which are not associated with His morality; they are omnipresence, omniscience, omnipotence, and immutability.

1. *Omnipresence.* This refers to the fact that God is present everywhere in and beyond the universe at the same time. This aspect of God is closely related to His immensity but has special significance to his presence within the universe (1 Kings 8:27).

   Whither shall I go from thy Spirit? or whither shall I flee from thy presence? If I ascend into

---

6   Ibid., 80.

> heaven, thou art there; if I make my bed in hell, behold thou art there. If I take the wings of the morning and dwell in the uttermost parts of the sea; even there shall thy hand lead me, and thy right hand shall hold me. If I say surely the darkness shall cover me; even the night shall be light about me. Yea the darkness hides not from thee; but the night shineth as the day; the darkness and the light are both alike to thee. (Ps. 139:7–12)

The doctrine of God's omnipresence is very comforting for the saint to know that our heavenly Father is always there with us in every situation (Matt. 28:20).

> Neither is there any creature that is not manifest in His sight; but all things are naked and opened unto the eyes of Him with whom we have to do. (Heb. 4:13)

It also causes us to exercise restraint, knowing that God is always watching and hearing us.

2. *Omniscience.* This refers to God's infinite knowledge of all things and beings in and beyond the boundaries of time. He knows Himself and everything about everyone from eternity past to eternity future. The doctrine of God's omniscience is evident in the design and intelligence of man, His creation; even the hairs on our head, God has serial-numbered (Matt. 10:30). God's infinite knowledge covers His complete knowledge of Himself— Father, Son, and Holy Spirit— His knowledge of all His creation, animate and inanimate, including the thoughts, hearts, works, needs, and wants of man, including all things about the future.

> O Lord thou hast searched me and known me. You know my down-sitting and mine up-rising, thou understand my thought afar off. You compass my path and my lying down and

art acquainted with all my ways. There is not a word in my tongue but lo, O Lord, you know it altogether. (Ps. 139:1–4)

Noteworthy is the fact that no one besides God has perfect knowledge of themselves and all things (Prov. 5:21; Acts 15:18).

3. *Omnipotence.* This refers to God's ability to do whatsoever He wills, for He is all-powerful. He is limited only by His nature, although with Him, nothing is impossible. He cannot deny Himself or lie and act contrary to His nature (Rev. 19:6).

If we believe not, yet He abides faithfully, He cannot deny Himself. (2 Tim. 2:13)

Wherein God willing more abundantly to shew unto the heirs of promise the immutability of His counsel, confirmed it by an oath. That by two immutable things in which it was impossible for God to lie, we might have a strong consolation, who have fled for refuge to lay hold upon the hope set before us. Which hope we have as an anchor of the soul, both sure and steadfast, and which enters that within the veil. (Heb. 6:17–19)

God is also somewhat limited with regard to His rational creatures, whom He allows to exercise their right of free will. God exercised His absolute power in the acts of creation, miracles, inspiration, regeneration, and immediate revelation and ordinate power in the manifestation of His permissive will, whereby the free will of His rational creatures are exercised (Acts 4:21–35). Further explanation on this aspect is provided with supporting scripture references in the closing statements on God's immutability hereafter. The devil and all demonic forces tremble before the everlasting God (Matt. 8:28–32).

Thou believe that there is one God; thou do well, the devils also believe and tremble. (James 2:19)

4. *Immutability.* This refers to the fact that God, whose perfection is absolute, cannot change in His essence, attributes, will, or consciousness. Change is expressed in an improvement or deterioration, but with God, this is impossible because His perfection is not only complete but infinitely absolute. Because He is perfect in wisdom, holiness, justice, love, mercy, and truth, God's plans and purposes cannot change. With Him, there is no variableness or shadow of turning (James 1:17). Thiessen states that God's immutability is due to His simplicity of essence, His self-existence and absolute perfection.[7] In His dealings with changing human beings, God, in His providence, grace, and mercy, makes adjustments like a loving Father to maintain His character and purposes.

Accordingly, His threats are often conditional as those made to Israel and Nineveh.

> And Moses besought the Lord his God and said Lord why doth thy wrath wax hot against thy people which thou hast brought forth out of the land of Egypt with great power and with a mighty hand. Wherefore should the Egyptians speak and say, for mischief did He bring them out to slay them in the mountains and to consume them from the face of the earth? Turn from thy fierce wrath and repent of this evil against thy people. Remember Abraham, Isaac, and Israel thy servants to whom thou swore by thine own self and said unto them I will multiply your seed as the stars of heaven and all this land that I have spoken of will I give unto your seed, and they shall inherit it forever. And the Lord repented of the evil which He thought to do unto His people. (Exod. 32:11–14)

> For word came unto the king of Nineveh and he arose from his throne, and he laid his robe from him and covered him with sackcloth and

---

7   Ibid., 83.

sat in ashes. And he caused it to be proclaimed and published through Nineveh by the decree of the king and his nobles saying, let neither man nor beast, herd nor flock taste anything; let them not feed nor drink water. But let man and beast be covered with sackcloth and cry mightily unto God; yea let them turn from his evil way and from the violence that is in their hands. Who can tell if God will turn and repent and turn away from His fierce anger that we perish not? And God saw their works that they turned from their evil way and God repented of the evil that He had said that He would do unto them, and He did it not. (Jonah 3:6–10)

Moral attributes. The qualities of God associated with His morality[8] are holiness, righteousness and justice, goodness, and truth.

1. *Holiness.* This refers to the fact that God is separated from and exalted far above all His creatures and moral evil. God's holiness is distinct from all His other attributes and can be viewed as the perfection of God in all that He is and a fundamental expression of His being and will. For this reason, holiness is the attribute God used mostly in the Old Testament in His self-disclosures (Josh. 24:19; Sam. 6:20; Isa. 40:25). He specially set boundaries around Mount Sinai when He descended there to speak to Moses. He divided the tabernacle and temple into holy and most holy places. He prescribed a special priesthood to mediate between Himself and the people of Israel. He prescribed special offerings for those persons who sought Him. He prescribed the many laws with regard to purification and for this reason. He also designated a special status to Israel among the nations of the world, referring to them as His people, a peculiar treasure unto Him above all people (Exod. 19:5–25; Exod. 26:33; Lev. 8–10; Lev. 11–15; Lev. 1–7; Num. 23:9).

---

8   Ibid., 84–88.

The scriptures teach three main things regarding God's holiness in relation to man: first, that Adam's sin separated the race of man from the Holy God; second, that man must approach God through the merits of Jesus Christ, God's foreordained lamb, who alone can atone for our sins; and third, that man must seek God with reverence and fear, (Hab. 1:13; Rom. 5:1–2; Eph. 2:18; Heb. 12:28; Isa. 6:5–7).

2. *Righteousness and justice.* God's righteousness and justice is exhibited in His dealings with man. He prescribed moral government upon the earth and imposed just laws with corresponding penalties for breaches. The ultimate Lawgiver executes His laws by the provision of rewards and punishments, that is, remunerative and punitive justice, where necessary (Deut. 7:9–13; Matt. 25:21). The believer is encouraged by God's righteous judgment, knowing that His righteous deeds will be rewarded while the evil deeds committed against him at the hand of the wicked will be met by God's wrath (Acts 17:31; Rev. 16:5–7).

3. *Goodness.* This aspect of God's attributes deals primarily with His permissive acts and responses toward His creatures and is exhibited in His love, benevolence, mercy, grace, and truth.

   a. *God's love.* The "agape" love of God is that perfection of His nature, which continually motivates Him to reach out to others with compassion and affection. His love is not impulsive but rational and voluntary and is exercised based on holiness, truth, and His will. The members of the Trinity are the primary objects of God's love, yet He chose to reach out to man and the universe in love. The scriptures attest to the love of God; He is called the God of love, Love, and the Initiator of love (2 Cor. 13:11; 1 John 4:8–10; John 3:16).

   b. *God's benevolence.* This aspect of God's attributes leads Him to deal generously, kindly, and carefully with all

His creatures. He exhibits concern for the welfare of His creatures (Matt. 6:26; Job 38:41; Psalm 104:21). His benevolence is not extended only to the righteous; it is extended to all mankind, the saved and unsaved alike (Matt. 5:45; Acts 14:17).

c. *God's mercy.* This refers to God's voluntary response to people in times of misery or distress; these acts of mercy are also referred to as God's compassion, loving-kindness, or pity. Noteworthy is the fact that candidates for mercy are always indebted or guilty of some transgression. The act of mercy reduces but does not altogether remove the debt or penalty (Eph. 2:4; James 5:11; 1 Peter 1:3; Psalm 103:17).

d. *God's grace.* This refers to God's goodness extended to undeserving persons, who are indebted or guilty of some offence. The act of grace, in this instance, removes the penalty or completely satisfies the debt, allowing the candidate to go free. The New Testament scriptures refer often to God's grace in superlative terms, such as "the glory of His grace," "surpassing riches of His grace," "manifold grace" (Eph. 1:6; Eph. 2:7; 1 Peter 4:10) respectively. God's grace is manifested toward the natural man in many ways: His forbearance and longsuffering through which He delays the penalty for sins, the distribution of talents and gifts to men, the provision of salvation, the provision of the Word of God, the gift and work of the Holy Spirit, and the influence of the righteous (Rom. 2:4; 9:22; 2 Peter 3:9; Heb. 6:7; 1 John 2:2; Hosea 8:12; John 16:8–11; Matt. 5:13) respectively. God's grace is also uniquely manifested toward His anointed people via their election, foreordination, redemption, salvation, sanctification, perseverance, service, and glorification (Eph. 1:4–6; Eph. 1:7; Acts 18:27; Rom. 5:21; 2 Cor. 12:9; Rom. 12:6; and 1 Peter 1:13) respectively.

e. *Truth.* God is not only the true God but also the Truth. All His knowledge, declarations, and representations attest to reality. His truth forms the foundation of all religions, knowledge, and wisdom; both scripture and nature affirm that God is genuine and true. Jesus declared that "God is the only true God" (John 17:3). God's truthfulness is also expressed in His faithfulness to perform all His promises and covenants (Deut. 7:9; Heb. 11:11; 1 Cor. 10:13).

Nature of God: Unity and Trinity

Unity of God

The doctrine of the unity of the Godhead is proclaimed repeatedly by God in the Old Testament and affirmed in the New Testament[9] by Jesus in His high-priestly prayer (Deut. 6:4; 4:35; John 17:11). The Bible consistently proclaims the fact that there is only one True and Living God, Jehovah, the God of Abraham, Isaac, and Jacob (1 Kings 8:60; Isa. 45:5; Mark 12:29–32; 1 Cor. 8:4–6). Unlike man, who is a compound being having material and immaterial parts, God is one infinite and perfect spirit being. He is indivisible. The unity of God, however, has no bearing on the fact that there are three persons in the Godhead; the divine nature permits the existence of personal distinctions. The divine nature remains numerically one forever.

Trinity

This refers to the mystery of the Godhead, three divine persons who are coequal and operate in perfect unity—God the Father, God the Son, and God the Holy Spirit—but eternally one infinite being and one God. The doctrine of the Trinity is supported by scripture, although the word *trinity* does not appear in the scriptures. The idea of three divine persons is evident in the Old and New Testaments.[10] In Genesis 19:24, a distinction is made between the angel of the Lord (this is a theophany of Jesus), who led Lot's family out of Sodom, and the Lord in heaven (this being God the Father). In Isaiah 48:16, a distinction is made between the divine persons. Jesus, speaking

---

9   Ibid., 89.
10   Ibid., 91–92.

through the prophet, states that the Father and the Spirit sent Him. In Matthew 28:19, Jesus commissioned the disciples to preach the gospel to all nations, baptizing them in the name of the Father and of the Son and of the Holy Spirit, clearly distinguishing between the members of the Godhead. At the baptism of Jesus recorded in Matthew 3:16–17, the three divine persons publicly convened: the Holy Spirit alighted on Christ's shoulder in the form of a dove, while God the Father burst the clouds announcing aloud that Jesus was His Beloved Son in whom He was well pleased. The distinction between the divine persons is consistent in the New Testament, especially in the apostle Paul's benediction, which concludes each of his epistles.

CHAPTER 2

CREATION OF THE ANGELS

The clause "In the beginning God created the heaven and the earth" (Gen. 1:1) refers to the beginning or creation of *chronos*, translated, "time." God exists in eternity, a state that is foreign to the race of man because our concept of life is shaped by time, space, place, and motion. Accordingly, our concept of eternity is not holistic and fluid but divided into eternity past, eternity present, and eternity future. All the ages of life of all beings and things have been and are current before the eyes of God, like a movie. Man's eternity past refers to the events that occurred prior to the creation of time. Eternity present refers to the events that occurred since the creation of time and those that will occur during the future generations of time, which, according to the prophetic Word of God, will conclude when God abolishes the curse of sin and death, creating the new heaven and earth wherein dwells righteousness (2 Peter 3:13; Rev. 21:1). That glorious act of God will introduce our eternity future, when all the saints of God will dwell and reign with Christ forever and ever (1 Cor. 15:26; Rev. 21–22).

God created Paradise, His dwelling place, and the angels prior to His creation of time, the heaven, and earth. The scriptures in both the Old and New Testaments affirm that there are several heavens. Several Old Testament scriptures indica te that God created more than one heaven. I will record a few here.

> Give ear O ye heavens, and I will speak, and hear
> O earth, the words of my mouth. (Deut. 32:1)

> He bowed the heavens also and came down; and
> darkness was under His feet. (Sam. 22:10)

> The heavens declare the Glory of God, and the
> firmament shows His handiwork. (Ps. 19:1)

Apostle Paul helps us to conclude that there are three heavens, for he states,

> I knew a man in Christ above fourteen years ago,
> whether in the body, I cannot tell, or whether out
> of the body, I cannot tell, God knows, such an one
> caught up to the third heaven How that he was
> caught up into Paradise, and heard unspeakable
> words, which it is not lawful for a man to utter.
> (2 Cor. 12:2, 4)

The first heaven is the atmospheric heaven, where the clouds are located and the birds and aircrafts fly; it is the heaven referred to in the following scriptures.

> And then the Lord's wrath be kindled against
> you, and He shut up the heaven, that there be no
> rain and that the land yield not her fruit; and lest
> ye perish quickly from off the good land which
> the Lord giveth you. (Deut. 11:17)

> Lord when thou went out of Seir when thou
> march out of the field of Edom, the earth
> trembled and the heavens dropped, the clouds
> also dropped water. (Judg. 5:4)

> Nevertheless, He left not Himself without
> witness, in that He did good, and gave us rain
> from heaven and fruitful seasons, filling our
> hearts with food and gladness. (Acts 14:17)

The second heaven is the celestial heaven, which is located above the atmospheric heaven and contains the sun, moon, stars, galaxies, asteroids, all the planets, outer space, and the satellites. It is the heaven referred to in the following scriptures.

For the stars of heaven and the constellations thereof shall not give their light; the sun shall be darkened in his going forth, and the moon shall not cause her light to shine. (Isa. 13:10)

And they shall spread them before the sun, and the moon and all the host of heaven, whom they have loved, whom they have served, and after whom they have walked, and whom they have sought, and whom they have worshipped: they shall not be gathered, nor be buried; they shall be for dung upon the face of the earth. (Jer. 8:2)

His going forth is from the end of the heaven, and his circuit unto the ends of it; and there is nothing hid from the heat thereof. (Ps. 19:6)

The third heaven is Paradise, the Dwelling Place of God, the heaven of heavens, and the place where God established His throne. It is the heaven referred to in the following Old and New Testament scriptures.

Enoch walked with God, and he was not, for God took him, Gen. 5:24. By faith Enoch was translated that he should not see death; and was not found, because God had translated him; for before his translation he had this testimony, that he pleased God. (Heb. 11:5)

And it came to pass, as they still went on and talked that behold there appeared a chariot of fire and horses of fire, and parted them both asunder, and Elijah went up by a whirlwind into heaven. (2 Kings 2:11)

After this manner therefore pray ye, Our Father which art in Heaven Hallowed be thy Name. (Matt. 6:9)

And Jesus said unto him, Verily I say unto thee, Today, shalt thou be with me in Paradise. (Luke 23:43)

And it came to pass, while He blessed them, he was parted from them and carried up into Heaven. (Luke 24:51)

And no man hath ascended to heaven, but he that came down from heaven, even the Son of man, which is in heaven. (John 3:13)

Jesus said unto her, touch me not for I am not yet ascended to my Father, but go to my brethren, and say unto them, I ascend unto my Father and your Father, and to my God and your God. (John 20:17)

But he being full of the Holy Ghost, looked up steadfastly into heaven, and saw the Glory of God and Jesus standing on the right hand of God. (Acts 7:55)

Nature of the Angels

In the light of the foregoing, people can discern that the clause in Genesis 1:1 refers to God's creation of the atmospheric and celestial heavens and the earth. I will now address the nature of the innumerable multitude of angels. The scriptures give no indication that the angels experienced childhood. They were all created as adults by the hand of our Lord and Savior Jesus Christ (Col. 1:16– 17). Many writers have addressed the subject of "angels" from time to time, but much of their conclusions conflict with the teachings of the scriptures. I fully endorse the views of Ron Graham, an Australian Bible preacher and teacher, conveyed in his article entitled "Cherubim and Seraphim Explained"[11] appended hereunder.

> Apostle's warning to Timothy is appropriate here "O Timothy guard what was committed to your trust. Avoid the profane and idle babbling and contradictions of what is falsely called knowledge. By professing it some have gone astray from the faith, 1 Tim. 6:20–21. The Bible certainly speaks of angels, but most of what is said today is not what the Bible says.
>
> For example, take the angelic hierarchy that are recited as though the list had Bible authority behind it. The ranking reads as follows from top to bottom, Cherubim, Seraphim, Thrones, Dominions, Lordships, Virtues or Strongholds, Powers or Authorities, Principalities or Rulers, Archangels and Angels. This list did not come from the Scriptures but from human thought. It seems odd that Angels and Archangels, whom we encounter in scripture are relegated to the bottom of the hierarchy. The human mind places its own inventions and speculations above the Word of God. I am aware that the Bible uses most of these words, however when we examine the places where those words are used; there is no indication that the writer is referring to ranks of angels, except for the Archangel and Angels. For example, Paul says that Christ created "all things in heaven and on earth, visible and invisible, whether thrones and dominions, or principalities, or powers. Col. 1:16. However, there is absolutely no reason to interpret this as the ranking of angels.

---

11   Ron Graham, Simplybible.com.

Now let's think about the Cherubim or Cherubs; the surprise here is that the Bible does not say that Cherubim are angels. Writers assume that they are angels, but no proof can be found in the scriptures. So let us examine the Cherubim/Cherub. After God drove Adam and Eve from the Garden of Eden, He stationed cherubim at the east of the Garden and a flaming sword which turned every way to guard the way to the tree of life, Gen. 3:24. We don't know how many there were, whether they were alive or what powers they had. To get more information we must move forward in the Bible to our next encounter with the cherubim.[12]

The next mention is found in God's instructions to Moses for the building of the Ark of the Covenant, Exodus 25:8–22. You shall make a mercy seat of pure gold. It shall be two and a half cubits long and one and a half cubits wide. And you shall make two cherubim of hammered gold. You shall make the cherubim at the two ends of the mercy seat; of one piece with the mercy seat shall you make the cherubim on its two ends. The cherubim shall spread out their wings above, to overshadow the mercy seat with their wings. The cherubim shall face each other, and their faces shall be toward the mercy seat.

If we stopped here and did not proceed to the next mention of cherubim in the Bible, we would say that they are carved images in the form of winged creatures. They have special significance in that they are positioned by God where His Glory and Power dwell. However,

---

12   Ibid.

there is a third instance of cherubim, that we need to examine before we draw our conclusions on this matter. This instance is the cherubim Ezekiel saw in his visions. The prophet Ezekiel describes his visions in vivid detail in chapters 1 and 10.

Behold a whirlwind came out of the north, and a great cloud, bright all around. Fire kept flashing from it; in the midst of the fire, there seemed to be gleaming metal. From within the cloud, there came the likeness of four living creatures. In appearance they were like humans, but each had four faces, and each of them had four wings. Their legs were straight, and the soles of their feet were like that of a calf's foot. Their feet shone like burnished bronze. Under all four wings they had human hands, Ezekiel 1:4–8. I observed the faces and wings of the four creatures. Their wings touched one another. The creatures went straight forward and did not turn. Each of the four creatures had a human face, and two wings covered its body. Each creature went straight forward, wherever the Spirit wished, so they went, yet without turning, Ezekiel 1:9–12.

In chapter 10, the prophet relates another vision involving the same living creatures,[13].

I beheld in the expanse above the heads of the cherubim, what looked like a throne made of sapphire. It was said to the man clothed in linen, "Go in among the whirling wheels underneath the cherubim. Fill your hands with burning coals from between the cherubim and scatter them over the city."

---

13   Ibid.

And so he did while I watched, Ezekiel 10:1–2.

Before continuing to share Pastor Graham's article, I wish to draw attention to the prophet Ezekiel's introduction to his prophecy: "As I was among the captives by the river of Chebar, the heavens were opened, and I saw visions of God" (Ezek. 1:1b). Ezekiel clearly outlined that what he saw were visions of God, not angels. Pastor Graham explains that

Ezekiel saw a vision which showed him signs; a sign does not signify itself but something else. For example, the sapphire throne in the vision Ezekiel 1:26; 10:1. represented the sovereignty of God, which the children of Israel scorned and rebelled against. Again, the prophet could not behold the shekinah Glory of God in its reality, so he recorded that he saw "the appearance of the likeness of the glory of the Lord" Ezekiel 1:28. In Solomon's temple the cherubim were beautiful carved images of olive wood overlaid with gold. They were, however, symbols; they portrayed the presence and mercy of God who can lift up the sinner. They did not portray any living being except God Himself; otherwise, they would be the very graven images forbidden in the ten commandments, Exodus 20:4. The cherubim that Ezekiel saw in the visions were also symbols; they appeared as living creatures, but they do not portray any living beings other than God and His attributes. For example, the creatures and wheels were full of eyes, it's not hard to understand that this represents God as all-wise, all-knowing, all-seeing. And the proceeding straight forward without turning symbolizes God's absolute righteousness and truth from which he never turns aside. The Bible records angels making appearances to human beings. For example, the archangel Gabriel was sent by God to a city of Galilee named Nazareth; he visited Mary, who became the mother of Jesus, Luke 1:26–28. This happened in the real world; it was not a symbolic vision; the angel was a real live angel. The Bible has no record of a real live cherub visiting and speaking to anyone, because there are no real live cherubs. Cherubs are images that represent God's presence and attributes, His goodness and severity, Rom. 11:22.

The Bible has little to say about the seraphim; the main passage is Isaiah's vision recorded at chapter 6. The vision states, In the year that king Uzziah died I saw the Lord sitting upon a throne high and lifted up and His robe filled the temple. Above Him stood the seraphim. Each had six wings, each covered his face with two wings, with two he covered his feet, and with two he flew. And one seraph called another and said Holy, Holy, Holy is the Lord of Hosts, the whole earth is full of His Glory! Isaiah 6:1–3. Then the doorposts shook at the voice of him who called, and the house was filled with smoke. And I said Woe is me! For I am undone! I am a man of unclean lips, and I dwell among people of unclean lips. I am lost because my eyes have seen the King, the Lord of Hosts! Isaiah 6:4–5. Then one of the seraphim flew to me having in his hand a burning coal that he had taken with tongs from the altar. And he touched my mouth and said Behold this has touched your lips, your guilt is taken away and your sin is atoned for. Isaiah 6:6–7.

Elsewhere in Isaiah we read Rejoice not O Philistia, all of you that the rod that struck you is broken, for from the serpent's root will come forth an adder, and its fruit will be a flying seraph, Isaiah 14:29 and 30:6. God used seraphim to punish the Israelites in the wilderness, then told Moses to make an image of a seraph and set it on a pole. God promised that anyone who was bitten could look at the bronze seraph and they would not die, Numbers 21:4–9. There is no support in scripture for teaching that seraphim are a class of angels. The passages we have examined are not about angelology; they do not inform us about angels but about the wisdom, power, glory, mercy, righteousness and grace of God. The Lord wants his children to believe and obey His Word so that He can grant them eternal blessings from His presence. Yes, He will punish rebellion, but it is His wish to provide atonement and welcome His children into His Presence.[14]

In summary, I endorse Pastor Graham's teaching that the scriptures reveal only two classes of angels—archangels and angels. Apostle Paul's use of the words *principalities*, *powers*, *rulers of darkness*, *thrones*, and *dominions* in Ephesians and Colossians respectively is a reference to the assignments or roles performed by the demons and is not intended to be a reference to their class. The archangels Gabriel and Michael made several appearances to the Lord's anointed servants throughout the Bible; noteworthy here is the fact that the third archangel, Lucifer, fell to the estate of Satan and was cast out of heaven when he decided to rebel against God to set up his own kingdom, the kingdom of darkness. Michael and the holy angels defeated him and his rebellious angels (Ish. 14: 12; Luke 10: 18). Michael intervened in the battle that ensued between the holy angels and the fallen angels from the kingdom of darkness, defeating them to permit Archangel Gabriel to provide

---

14   Ibid.

the revelation Daniel sought to his vision (Dan. 10:13; 12:1). This text indicates that the angels were assigned to protect the nation of Israel, an assignment evident from Israel's deliverance from the Egyptian bondage and pilgrimage through the wilderness to the Promised Land of Canaan (Exodus).

The angels were created as very skilled warriors; all the holy angels are superior warriors to those who rebelled with Satan, losing relationship with their original source. The text also indicates that God used the angels to provide revelation and illumination to His anointed servants in the Old Testament prior to the day of Pentecost, when the church received the gift of the Holy Spirit. Archangel Michael appeared in scripture contending with Satan over the body of Moses after his death. It is apparent that Satan claimed the body because, at that time, he had the keys to death and hell. But God Himself buried Moses's body and hid it from the devil, a created being who operates with knowledge and power delegated to him by God (Deut. 34:4–6; Jude 1:9; Heb. 2:14).

Archangel Gabriel was sent to the elderly priest Zacharias to announce the miraculous birth of his son, John the Baptist, Jesus's forerunner. Discerning doubt on the part of Zacharias, the angel revealed that he stood in the very presence of God the Father and struck the priest dumb until the prophecy was fulfilled before his eyes (Luke 1; 11–20). Gabriel also visited the Virgin Mary to announce that God chose her to bear His son, the Christ child, whose incarnation was prophesied in the Old Testament scriptures (Isa. 7:14; 9:6–7; Mic. 5:2). Unlike Zacharias, Mary gladly received the tidings conveyed by the angel, consenting "Behold the handmaid of the Lord; be it unto me according to thy word" (Luke 1:26–38). Gabriel, together with a multitude of angels, visited a company of shepherds who were attending their sheep in the countryside of the city of Bethlehem, announcing to them the glorious news of the birth of the Christ child.

> The angel said unto them, Fear not for behold I bring you good tidings of great joy, which shall be to all people. For unto you is born this day in the city of David a Savior, which is Christ the Lord. And this shall be a sign unto you; Ye shall find the babe wrapped in swaddling clothes lying in a

manger. And suddenly there was with the angel a multitude of the heavenly host praising God saying, Glory to God in the highest and on earth peace, good will toward men. (Luke 2:9–14)

I mentioned earlier in this chapter that God created the angels prior to His creation of the earth. They were created spirit beings without sex organs and do not marry or reproduce after their kind (Luke 20:34–36). They cannot die and derive their knowledge and power from God their Creator. The angels are intelligent beings; their knowledge and strength grossly exceed that of human beings (2 Sam. 14:20; Matt. 24:36). However, they are not omnipresent, omnipotent, or omniscient. The angels have a will and were created volitional beings to worship and serve the True and Living God (Father, Son, and Holy Spirit), but that choice was exercised, once and for all, when Lucifer rebelled against God. Noteworthy is the fact that the fallen angels are inferior to the holy angels because they lost their connection to their source and Creator (Luke 10:17–20; Rev. 20:1–2). Accordingly, the estate of all the angels is sealed; the fallen angels, now referred to as demons, have already been condemned to eternal damnation in hell (Isa. 14:12– 15; Jude 1:6; 2 Peter 2:4).

God, in His foreknowledge, created an innumerable multitude of angels, too numerous to be numbered. They are emotional beings and exhibit a keen interest in the affairs of men, in particular, God's relationship with the saints. They express joy and excitement in worshipping the Lord and conveying glad tidings to God's servants (Job 38:7). Contrary to the belief of many saints, the scriptures do not indicate that angels possess wings. They are spirit beings and do not need wings to fly; gravity has no hold on spirit beings. Many instances in both the Old and New Testaments record that the angels who visited the servants of God had the appearance of normal male human beings; it is for this reason we are exhorted to be careful when entertaining strangers, lest we encounter angels unawares (Heb. 13:2). I outlined earlier in this chapter that in the instances in scripture where the narrative mentioned angels having wings, the writers were sharing a vision using metaphoric language. Live angels appeared to Abraham, Hagar, Lot, Jacob, Moses, Joshua, Mary, Zacharias, the shepherds,

Mary Magdalene, Mary the mother of James, Salome, and all the apostles at Jesus's ascension; the scriptures clearly indicate that none of them possessed wings.

Angels' Relationship with God

God, the very personification of love, chose to call Himself, God the Father. This status conveys the mindset of our God; all the attributes of the Godhead can be seen in this concept. God made the race of man the object of His great love, grace, and mercy, and in so doing, He plans with family and relationship in mind. True love can only be effectively expressed in a relationship. Everything God plans, purposes, does, and says is with love, protection, provision, growth, development, justice, lovingkindness, righteousness, restoration, and renewal in mind.

> God said, let us make man in our image and after our likeness, and let them have dominion over the fish of the sea, and over the fowl of the air, and over the cattle, and over all the earth, and over every creeping thing that creep upon the earth. So, God created man in His own image, and in the image of God He created him, male and female He created them. And God blessed them, and God said unto them be fruitful and multiply and replenish the earth, and subdue it, and have dominion over the fish of the sea, and over the fowl of the air, and over every living thing that move upon the earth. (Gen. 1:26–28)

> Thus saith the Lord, let not the wise man glory in his wisdom, neither let the mighty man glory in his might, let not the rich man glory in his riches; but let him that glory, glory in this that he understands and know me, that I am the Lord which exercise lovingkindness, judgment and righteousness in the earth; for in these things I delight, saith the Lord. (Jer. 9:23–24)

> But if the wicked will turn from all his sins that he had committed and keep all my statutes and

do that which is lawful and right he shall surely live, he shall not die. All his transgressions that he hath committed, they shall not be mentioned unto him, in his righteousness that he hath done he shall live. Have I any pleasure at all that the wicked should die? Saith the Lord God, and not that he should return from his ways and live? (Ezek. 18:21–23)

The members of the Godhead share all the attributes of deity nevertheless; they utilize the services of their angels to accomplish assignments in the affairs of the race of man, saved and unsaved (Heb. 1:14). God the Father has an open relationship with His angels, who appear before Him frequently to receive assignments of ministry on earth; Jesus Himself received such ministry after His temptation.

Take heed that ye despise not one of these little ones, for I say unto you that in heaven their angels do always behold the face of my Father which is in heaven. (Matt. 18:10)

Then said Jesus unto him, get thee hence Satan for it is written, thou shall worship the Lord thy God, and Him only shall thou serve. Then the Devil left him and behold angels came and ministered to Him. (Matt. 4:10–11)

Other instances where the Lord used angels to do His bidding are appended hereunder.

And when the angel stretched out his hand upon Jerusalem to destroy it, the Lord repented Him of the evil, and said to the angel that destroyed the people, it is enough; stay now thy hand. (2 Sam. 24:16)

And the man that stood among the myrtle trees answered and said, these are they whom the Lord hath sent to walk to and fro through the earth. And they answered the angel of the Lord that stood among the myrtle trees and said we have walked to and fro through the earth and behold all the earth sit still and is at rest. (Zech. 1:10–11)

For the Son of man shall come in the glory of His Father with His angels; and then He shall reward every man according to his works. (Matt. 16:27)

Think thou that I cannot now pray to my Father, and He shall presently give me more than twelve legions of angels. (Matt. 26:53)

And the angel answering said unto him, I am Gabriel that stand in the presence of God, and am sent to shew you these glad tidings. (Luke 1:19)

And immediately the angel of the Lord smote him because he gave not God the Glory; and he was eaten of worms and gave up the ghost. (Acts 12:23)

Finally, I wish to address the fallacy embraced by some scholars concerning the following scripture text.

That the sons of God saw the daughters of men that they were fair; and they took them wives of all which they choose. (Genesis 6:2)

Some theologians and scholars interpret the phrase "sons of God" to refer to angels, but angels have never been called by that phrase anywhere in the scriptures. The term "sons of God" always referred to prophets, other anointed servants of God, or believers in Christ, generally. I will demonstrate this by a careful examination of many such phrases in the Bible.

For centuries, theologians have been speculating about the identity of the sons of God referred to in both the Old and New Testaments. The first mention appears in Genesis 6:2. The Jews were instructed not to intermarry with Gentiles; you will recall that Samson violated this rule when he married Delilah, a decision that led to his demise. The apostle Paul admonishes us as believers not to marry unbelievers, for what fellowship does light have with darkness? There are two schools of thought regarding the text. The first states that the sons of God were fallen angels, but that could not be possible since the Bible clearly establishes that angels have no reproductive organs. The second school of thought, which I affirm, states that the sons of God were the descendants of Seth, Adam's son. The text is conveying that some of these men of God chose wives who were descendants of Cain. You need to know what transpired before that time since it explains why they were called sons of God.

The scriptures record that Seth was born to Adam and Eve after the death of Abel and had a heart like unto his deceased brother, Abel, to seek after the Lord. The miracle of his firstborn son, Enos, so inspired Seth to the extent that he became the first true evangelist and caused many to turn from sin to call on the name of the Lord (Gen. 4:25–26). We see this very miracle occurring again with Enoch, whose life and ministry was transformed on the birth of his son Methusclah (Gen. 5:22–24; Heb. 11:5). The heart of Enoch was so pure that the Lord took him to heaven; he was the first man to be translated into heaven, escaping death. The sons of God were great evangelists who declared the counsel of God in that era.

Noteworthy is the astonishing decrease in the life expectancy of the race of man from Genesis chapter 5 to chapter 6. Because of the rapid increase of evil in the earth and the corruption of the heart of men, God reduced their life expectancy from seven hundred years to one hundred and twenty. And when the book of Psalms was written it was further reduced to seventy years (Gen. 6:3; Ps. 90:10).

One of the most popular uses of the term "sons of God" appears at Job 1:6, "Now there was a day when the sons of God came to present themselves before the Lord, and Satan came also among them." Again, there are two schools of thought on the identity of the sons of God here and the venue of the meeting or convention. Some theologians believe these were angels who met with God in the second heaven since Satan cannot enter God's dwelling place, Paradise. I refute this theory for two reasons. First, God installed Adam, a man, as His legal representative on earth and not the angels. Second, the angels are ministering servants sent forth by God to minister to His anointed servants on earth regarding the administration of His kingdom on earth.

It is my firm belief that this text was referring to a special meeting or convention of the leaders of God's people at that time in history to confer and agree on important matters of God's business. Noteworthy is the fact that whenever and wherever the saints gather for a service or church business, they present themselves before the Lord (Matt. 18:20; Heb. 12:18–24). The early church fathers met regularly to confer and resolve complex issues that were before the church, examples the Councils of Nicaea in AD 325 and that of Ephesus in AD 431.

Another appearance of the phrase "sons of God" is in Romans 8:18–23. Genesis 6:5–7 and 9:12–15 provides a background for this text. The moral depravity of the heart of man was so gross that every imagination of their heart was evil continually; it caused God to regret that He created man, and grieved His heart to the core. In judgment, God destroyed every living thing on the earth consequent on man's rebellion. Genesis 9 relates the rainbow covenant God made with man, the earth, and every living creature on earth, never to judge by water again. Accordingly, the text in Romans refers to the restitution of all things through Christ in the future eternal state. In other New Testament uses of the term, believers in Christ are referred to as sons of God. These are the following.

> As many as receive Him, to them gave He power to become the sons of God, even to them that believe on His Name. (John 1:12)

> That ye be blameless and harmless, the sons of God, without rebuke, in the midst, of a crooked and perverse nation. (Phil. 2:15)

CHAPTER 3

GOD'S MOTIVATION FOR THE CREATION OF MAN

It is important to note that Satan and his rebellious angels were defeated and cast out of heaven before the creation of man. The holy angels exhausted the use of their free will and had no ability to reproduce after their kind to award their Creator another generation of holy servants. The two primary reasons God created mankind was for fellowship and to receive glory (1 John 1:3; 1 Cor. 10:31). "Even everyone that is called by my name; for I have created him for my Glory, I have formed him yea I have made him" (Isa. 43:7). God's plan for Adam and Eve was for them to take on His righteous nature and acquire a good character by their obedience. Their obedience would have resulted in an elevation in their relationship and fellowship to a right standing before God. They already spent time with God in the garden in the cool of the day, but that was just lunch and was designed by God to be a motivation for a greater and deeper fellowship and intimacy.

I will use the testimony of two witnesses, Enoch and Elijah, on this matter. Enoch walked with God at a time when there were no written scriptures, just the natural revelation of God in nature (Gen. 5:21–24 and Heb. 11:5). Remember, this Holy God cannot condone sin, yet He found this man to be so perfect in character that He could not get enough of his fellowship. Next, I will examine the testimony of the prophet Elijah, who confronted the eight hundred and fifty prophets of Baal and killed them on Mount Carmel after proving to the nations that Jehovah was the only Living God (1 Kings 18:19–40). He gave himself fully to the service of God although he had a family. Elijah also reestablished the school of prophets, first established by Samuel to overcome corruption in the nation, teaching young men to seek after the righteousness of God and live lives of service to Him (2 Kings 2:11). The Lord enjoyed the company of these men so much that He decided to promote them to live with Him fulltime in heaven; they were translated into heaven, escaping death.

God made man in His image and after His likeness to meet His need for fellowship and worship. He made the race of man for Himself. "It is in Him we live, move, and have our being" (Acts 17:28a). Most people don't know that this experience people call life on earth is not the real life of man in God's mindset; it's only the selection process. The life God prepared for man is eternal life through Jesus Christ, when, in the fullness of time, believers shall live and reign with Him forever. That's why Jesus told Nicodemus, "You must be born again, what is born of the flesh is flesh and what is born of the Spirit is spirit" (John 3:5–6). To experience this life, people must do better than Adam and Eve. Adam had the power not only to intervene and prevent Eve from picking the fruit but to cast Satan out of the garden. God instructed Adam to take dominion and subdue anything that sought to violate the laws of God, but he failed to use his authority to subdue the devil and became a slave to him (Gen. 1:28; Rom. 5:12).

King Solomon provides a glimpse of God's wisdom, joy, admiration, and glory of His creative work on earth from the race of man.

> Except the Lord build the house, they labor in vain that build it, except the Lord keep the city, the watchman wake but in vain. Lo children are a heritage of the Lord; and the fruit of the womb is His reward. As arrows are in the hand of a mighty man, so are children of the youth. (Ps. 127:1, 3–4)

The Lord provided a record of His wisdom, His knowledge of mankind, and His provision to meet their every need on the earth in the Garden of Eden experience (Gen. 1:1–31). It is God who provides the race of man the knowledge, wisdom, and understanding to build and secure houses, businesses, cities, and every endeavor necessary to protect the welfare of every community. He progressively releases knowledge, wisdom, and understanding to mankind in every generation in accordance with His divine program and purposes.

The glory of God's presence is evident everywhere in Paradise, the gem of the spiritual realm. I am using the word *glory* here to capture the sum total of the attributes of God. God desired to see evidence of His glory, likewise in the material realm of the earth. That assignment could not be accomplished by the angels for a few reasons, the most important of which is they were not created to dwell and operate in the material earthly realm. Second, God wanted the glory of His presence to be seen and understood by mankind in every generation; that assignment could not be accomplished by the angels for the aforementioned reason—they are spirit beings.

God's Desire and Aspiration for Man

God's desire is for man to utilize their gifts and talents for positive purposes and not for evil purposes as those exhibited by the generation that experienced the judgment of the flood.

> And God saw that the wickedness of man was
> great in the earth, and that every imagination of
> the thoughts of his heart was only evil continually.
> And it repented the Lord that He had made man
> on the earth, and it grieved Him at His heart.
> (Gen. 6:5–8)

The Lord commanded the nation of Israel to fear Him and raise their children in the fear and admonition of His divine counsel.

> Thou shall love the Lord thy God with all thine
> heart, and with all thy soul, and with all thy
> might. And these words which I command thee
> this day shall be in thy heart: and thou shall teach
> them diligently unto thy children and shall talk
> of them when thou sit in thy house and when
> thou walk by the way and when thou lie down

and when thou rise. And thou shall bind them for a sign upon thy hand, and they shall be as frontlets between thy eyes. And thou shall write them upon the posts of thy house and on thy gates. (Deut. 6:5–9)

The Jews were commanded not only to live holy lives but to envelop their homes with the counsel and fragrance of God's presence. Both parents were instructed to teach their children the counsel of God from the time of their birth. God takes great pleasure in the birth, nurture, growth, and development of the children of His people, lives groomed in the fear of God like young Samuel, David, Shadrack, Meshack, Abednego, and Daniel. Apostle Paul also provides evidence that God orchestrated the glorious plan of redemption to display His manifold wisdom before the eyes of men, the holy angels, and the demonic beings.

And to make all men see, what is the fellowship of the mystery which from the beginning of the world had been hid in God, who created all things by Jesus Christ. To the intent that now unto the principalities and powers in heavenly places might be known by the church the manifold wisdom of God. According to the eternal purpose which He purposed in Christ Jesus our Lord. (Ephesians 3:9–11)

The psalmist King David records the fact that the might, majesty, and glory of God is clearly displayed to all via natural revelation. He also refers to the conduct of those in positions of authority who chose to resist the purposes of God and proceed to attack the anointed servants of God.

The heavens declare the Glory of God, and the firmament show His handiwork. Day unto day utters speech and night u not night show knowledge. There is no speech nor language where their voice is not heard. Their line is gone out through all the earth, and their words to the end of the world. (Ps. 19:1–4)

Why do the heathen rage, and the people imagine a vain thing? The kings of the earth set themselves, and the rulers take counsel together against the Lord and against His anointed, saying let us break their bands asunder and cast away their cords from us. He that sits in the heavens shall laugh; the Lord shall have them in derision. Then shall He speak unto them in His wrath and vex them in His sore displeasure. (Ps. 1:1–5)

A careful examination of the dialogue of the members of the Godhead recorded in Genesis 1:26–28 reveals God's aspiration for the race of man. I will elaborate in detail God's desire concerning mankind by outlining the differences God employed in His creation of man vis-à-vis His creation of the angels.

1. Man was made in God's image and likeness; the angels were not.

2. Man was given the ability to reproduce after his kind; the angels were not.

3. Man was created a spirit being with a material clay body to dwell on earth; the angels were not.

4. Man may exercise the volition of free will throughout his life on earth; the angels had only one opportunity to choose their allegiance.

5. Believers in Christ have the covenant promise to rule and reign with Christ Jesus in His kingdom after the rapture; the angels do not have such a promise.

Be Fruitful and Multiply

In blessing the race of man, He created in His image and likeness. God made the declaration that He had equipped them to be fruitful and multiply. Noteworthy is the fact that God was speaking from His concept of fruitfulness, evident in the fruit of the Spirit, listed by apostle Paul: "The fruit of the Spirit is love, joy, peace, longsuffering, gentleness, goodness, faith, meekness, and temperance" (Gal. 5:22–23). Adam and Eve were created in a state of innocence and had the opportunity to turn their innocence into righteousness by their obedience to the righteous commandments of God. In other words, they had the opportunity to build their character from the infant stage of innocence to that of a right standing with God.

God creates by speaking. He said, "Let there be light and there was light" (Gen. 1:3). The text Genesis 1:28, including the phrase "be fruitful and multiply," was both a command and the expressed desire of God for mankind. He was addressing the character of man by use of the phrase "be fruitful." Character defines the nature of relationships an individual can and will establish in life. It also determines that person's usefulness and productivity to God and man, church, family, community, and society at large. Jesus speaking to the disciples addressed this topic, saying,

> Abide in me and I in you, as the branch cannot bear fruit of itself, except it abide in the vine; no can you, except you abide in me. I am the vine, and you are the branches. He that abides in me and I in him the same bringeth forth much fruit, for without me you can do nothing. Herein is my Father glorified, that you bear much fruit; so, shall you be my disciples. (John 15:4–5, 8)

God created Adam and Eve as adults but created them with sex organs and the ability to reproduce after their kind. The ability to reproduce, however, was and is not based in the body of man, as many persons think. I will illustrate by referring to household electrical appliances. They are manufactured with the ability to perform specific tasks; however, they are useless until we plug them into the power source and turn the power button on. Likewise, God is involved in the life of every human being. Examine the way He speaks about His care for the animals and plants.

> Behold the fowls of the air, for they sow not, neither do they reap, nor gather into barns, yet your heavenly Father feeds them. Are you not

much better than them? Which of you, by taking thought can add one cubit to his stature? And why take thought for raiment? Consider the lilies of the field, how they grow, how they toil not, neither do they spin. And yet I say unto you that even Solomon in all his glory was not arrayed like one of these. (Matt. 6:26–29)

God is conveying in this text that His care for man far exceeds His care for the animals and plants. Two other texts convey the level of God's involvement in the life of mankind.

But even the hairs of your head are all numbered. Fear not therefore, you are of more value than many sparrows. (Luke 12:7)

O Lord, thou hast searched me and known me. You know my down-sitting and my uprising, you understand my thoughts afar off. (Ps. 139:1–2)

The first text records the fact that God has serial-numbered every grain of hair on the heads of mankind. That should not amaze anyone because the scriptures tell us that He calls the billions of stars by name (Ps. 147:4). The second text indicates that the omnipresent and omniscient God knows all the thoughts of men before they experience them.

The scriptures indicate that it is the spirit that produces life, and God is the person who brings about conception by sending forth His life-giving spirit (Ps. 104:30; Isa. 42:5b; Ezek. 18:4). The Old Testament has many examples of God's involvement in the fertility and the progeny of individuals and families. I will mention a few here.

Neither shall thy name any more be called Abram, but thy name shall be Abraham; for a father of many nations have I made thee. And I will make thee exceedingly fruitful, and I will make nations of thee, and kings shall come out of thee. (Gen. 17:5–6)

> But unto Hannah he gave a worthy portion for he loved Hannah; but the Lord had shut up her womb. And she was in bitterness of soul and prayed unto the Lord and wept sore. And she vowed a vow and said, O Lord of hosts if thou will indeed look on the affliction of thy handmaid and remember me and not forget thy handmaid but will give unto thy handmaid a man child then I will give him unto the Lord all the days of his life and there shall no razor come upon his head. Wherefore it came to pass when the time was come about after Hannah had conceived, that she bare, a son and called his name Samuel saying because I have asked him of the Lord. (1 Sam. 1:5–6, 20)

> And the Lord visited Hannah so that she conceived and bare three sons and two daughters. (1 Sam. 2:21)

> And the Lord turned the captivity of Job, when he prayed for his friends; also, the Lord gave Job twice as much as he had before. He also had seven sons and three daughters. (Job 42:10, 13)

The first text is the familiar story of God's restoration of the vitality of life to his servants Abraham and Sarah, who had passed their child-bearing age. History records the faithfulness of God in keeping His covenant with Abraham and his seed in every generation. The second text displayed God's involvement in withholding Hannah's fertility to create a desperate pursuit and righteous discernment of His needs. God rewarded her diligence with five children after the birth of Samuel, who was given to the Lord's service according to the vow she made before the Lord. The final text deals with the Lord's involvement in the life and tribulations of Job. God was very proud of this righteous man's dedication and decided to enter a challenge with the devil to try his faith. Contrary to the accusations of his friends, Job's affliction was not a result of God's displeasure but His pleasure (Job 1:8–12).

CHAPTER 4

THE CREATION OF MAN

The narrative on the creation of man is provided at the beginning of the Bible in the book of Genesis.

> The Lord God formed man of the dust of the ground and breathed into his nostrils the breath of life; and man became a living soul. (Gen. 2:7)

From the account of the writer, Moses, the reader can picture the clay body of Adam lying lifeless on the ground until God breathed into his nostrils His life-giving spirit. The prophet Isaiah provides some insight into the creative work of God.

> Thus saith God the Lord, He that created the heavens, and stretched them out; He that spread forth the earth; and that which cometh out of it; He that giveth breath unto the people upon it and spirit to them that walk therein. (Isa. 42:5)

This text indicates that God placed two things simultaneously into the body of Adam, his spirit and his soul. Apostle James recorded that the body of man has no life of its own, for the body without the spirit is dead (James 2:26). Prior to the actual creation of Adam, the members of the Godhead held a conference and decided to create man in their image and after their likeness.

And God said, let us make man in our image after our likeness and let them have dominion over the fish of the sea, and over the fowl of the air, and over the cattle, and over all the earth and over every creeping thing that creep upon the earth. So, God created man in His own image, in the image of God created He him; male and female created He them. (Gen. 1:26–27)

The Image and Likeness of God

Genesis records that God made man in His own image and after His own likeness. However, God, unlike man, has no material body. *Image* refers to the general nature or structure of God, who is triune, three co-equal persons—Father, Son, and Holy Spirit— who occupy one spiritual body (Deut. 6:4; John 14:11). Hence, this likeness evident in man cannot be physical. Accordingly, I will outline hereunder four categories wherein persons may detect the image and likeness God gave Adam and Eve at creation, namely image, moral, mental, and social likeness.

Image. Man, like God, possesses three elements: spirit, soul, and body. Apostle Paul, in his prayer, referred to these components: "And the very God of peace sanctify you wholly; and I pray God your whole spirit and soul and body be preserved blameless unto the coming of our Lord Jesus Christ" (1 Thess. 5:23). I will address the nature and functions of each of these components in the following section on the constitution of man.

Moral likeness. Before Adam sinned, he shared the righteousness of God. He was in perfect health, not subject to death or diseases of any sort. God designed man with this constitution because man was made to fellowship with Him, in whose presence no sin can enter. A biblical view of man's character will be incomplete if no mention is made of his eternal destiny. The soul of man will never die; the believer is destined to spend eternity in the presence of God, while the persons who die in their sins will spend eternity in hell (John 11:25–26; Heb. 9:27; Rev. 21:7–8). The advent of *pasha* marred this aspect of man's constitution, but praise God, a way was provided by Jesus to redeem individuals from the fall and restore them to a right relationship with their Creator. (Eph. 4:24; Rom. 8:29–30; John 3:3). By regeneration, the believer is restored to that state of moral likeness in Jesus Christ.

> For if any man be in Christ, he is a new creature;
> behold all things are become new. (2 Cor. 5:17)

Mental likeness. Because God intended for man to have communion with Him, He gave him a nature like His own nature— that is, He made him a rational, moral, free agent. By so doing, God made man far superior to all the other inhabitants of the earth. These characteristics equipped man with the faculty to sense, understand, and know God personally. Of course, no one can sense God on his own, but God made man for Himself, much like a receiving device, the radio or television, is designed to receive communication signals. So God communicates and reveals Himself to man via the person of the Holy Spirit, the written and spoken Word of God, which inspires faith and the disposition of prayer. The writer of the Epistle to the Hebrews announced that it is impossible for anyone to please God without faith. The patriarchs of old, some of whose names are recorded in Hebrews 11, all lived in that supernatural mental state of faith before they finally died and were received in heaven by the Lord of glory, in person, (1 Cor. 2:12–16; Heb. 11:6, 13; Phil. 4:7–8).

Social likeness. God has a social nature and designed man with this aspect of His nature so that man would seek Him and find completion and fulfillment in Him (Col. 2:10; Acts 17:27–28). God the Father delights in fellowship and worship. He has fellowship with the other members of the Trinity, the angelic hosts, and man, mortal and immortal, in varying levels of fellowship. God's sovereign rule of the universe is without question. Likewise, He gave man a charge to take dominion over the earth as His representative and adorned him with a helpmeet in woman. Man is required by God to honor responsibilities at varying levels—spiritual, civil, and social—while maintaining loving and nurturing relationships as good stewards, first with Him as God, then with his spouse, his fellow man/woman, at every level of government, business, society, and the environment (Gen. 1:28; Luke 12:42; 1 John 4:7–8).

The Constitution of Man

I define man as a soul, that has a spirit and lives in a body. To be precise, what we see in the mirror is the house in which we live, because the essential component of man is his soul. The Lord, speaking through the prophet Ezekiel, said, "Behold, all souls are mine, as the soul of the father, so also the soul of the son is mine, and the soul that sins it shall die" (Ezek. 18:4). This text records God's claim to every human being and communicates that it is the soul of man that makes choices in life; it is the soul that sins, and it is the soul He will judge. Jesus endorsed this position when He inquired, "What shall it profit a man if he gains the whole world and loses his own soul? or what shall a man give in exchange for his soul?" (Mark 8:36–37). The reader may also glean this truth by examining what happens when a man dies. Solomon records, "Then shall the dust return to the earth as it was, and the spirit shall return unto God who gave it" (Eccl. 12:7). Apostle Paul affirms that the three elements of man are spirit, soul, and body (1 Thess. 5:23). The endeavor here is to determine the essential component of man; by the process of elimination, one can conclude that the main element, the real person, is not the body or the spirit, but the soul.

Apostle James, the brother of Jesus, recorded some pro-found truths in his brief epistle. I wish to refer to two of these currently. First, he states that the body of man has no life of its own. It is energized by the spirit and dies when God withdraws the spirit (James 2:26). This truth is endorsed by the psalmist King David: "Thou take away their breath they die, and return to their dust" (Ps. 104:29b). Second, James records that the demons believe that there is only one true God. "You believe that there is one God, thou do well, the devils also believe and tremble" (James 2:19). I will now address the nature and functions of each element of man.

Spirit of Man

The spirit of man is the most important element of man because it is the component that produces "God consciousness." It is the element via which God communicates with man, providing guidance and direction. It is the temple and dwelling place of the Holy Spirit in the life of the believer. The spirit is in the abdomen or belly and is invisible

(John 7:38; Prov. 20:27). The function of the spirit is threefold: worship, intuition, and conscience.

Worship. Jesus, speaking to the Samaritan woman, said, "The hour cometh and now is when the true worshipers shall worship the Father in spirit and in truth; for the Father seek such to worship Him. God is a Spirit and they that worship Him must worship Him in spirit and in truth" (John 4:23–24). The believer serves the Lord effectively based on His Word of Truth via the fellowship of the Holy Spirit and enters a spiritual and emotional experience in heavenly places during worship (Rom. 1:9; 7:6; 8:16).

Intuition. The Holy Spirit imparts knowledge, wisdom, and understanding to believers to guide and direct them in life and ministry. This method of communication includes thoughts, imaginations, ideas, dreams, and illumination of the scriptures (Prov. 20:27; Ps. 18:28; Acts 18:5; 1 Cor. 2:11).

Conscience. The Holy Spirit uses this medium to equip people, saved and unsaved, to judge circumstances, thoughts, imaginations, and spirits (Prov. 20:27; Rom. 8:16; 2 Tim. 1:7; Ps. 51:10). Many theologians and scholars state that the conscience is a function of the soul of man, but that position contradicts the teaching of the scriptures. Apostle Paul records,

> Because the carnal mind is enmity against God; for it is not subject to the law of God, neither indeed can be **and** I find then a law that, when I would do good, evil is present with me. For I delight in the law of God after the inward man; but I see another law in my members, warring against the law of my mind, and bringing me into captivity to the law of sin, which is in my members. (Rom. 8:7; 7:21–23)

The soul and flesh of man was corrupted by sin and became agents of the kingdom of darkness, consistently resisting the counsel and purposes of God (Rom. 3:23; 11:32; Gal. 5:17). Theologians examining the progression of our inborn sin nature observed a deterioration from missing the mark of God's requirement to trespassing, which may be intentional or unintentional, then to willful, premeditated decisions to violate the laws of God without repentance. This ultimate stage is referred to as iniquity. They have difficulty resolving the contrasting behavior of an individual over an extended period and were reluctant to assign the function of conscience to the spirit. However, there is a biblical explanation for the deteriorating conduct of persons who consistently defy the promptings of their conscience.

> Likewise reckon also, yourselves to be dead indeed unto sin, but alive unto God through Jesus Christ our Lord. Let not sin therefore reign in your mortal body, that you should obey it in the lusts thereof. Neither yield your members as instruments of unrighteous-ness unto sin; but yield yourselves unto God as those that are alive from the dead, and your members as instruments of righteousness unto God. For sin shall not have dominion over you; for you are not under the law but under grace. What then? Shall we sin because we are not under the law, but under grace? God forbid. Know you not that to whom you yield yourselves servants to obey, his servants you are to obey, whether of sin unto death, or of obedience unto righteousness? (Rom. 6:11–16)

This is the process whereby people who once lived normal lives have undergone drastic character changes, being influenced by friends or relatives to indulge in destructive practices, such as drug abuse, gambling, prostitution, criminal activity, and homosexuality and are now different altogether. When a person continues to practice iniquity— that is, choosing to sin without a desire to repent—they violate their conscience, the firewall protection God gave them to warn them of the danger of destructive actions. This course of action causes their conscience to malfunction, being seared, and shift from a protective mode to a defensive mode, whereby it seeks to defend the person's sinful behavior. This switch takes place because God will not violate the will of individuals. He will not force anyone to do anything they don't want to do. Those persons require intercession for deliverance from the strongholds of the devil, for with God, all things are possible to them that believe (Mark 9:23). The spirit of the unsaved person is dead or unresponsive to the things of God but may be quickened by the Holy Spirit when that person in faith seeks God and responds to the gospel, surrendering their life to Christ (John 3:5–6; Rom. 10:9–10).

Soul of Man

This element produces self-consciousness and is the real person. It is spiritual in nature and, like the spirit, came from the mouth of God and can only experience true growth and development by a personal relationship with God (Ezek. 18:4; Matt. 4:4; John 1:4, 9). The soul, though spiritual in nature, takes the shape of the body and fits into it, like a hand in a glove. It comprises the will, mind, and emotions of man.

Will. This is the faculty of volition, the power and process of making rational choices or controlling one's own actions and destiny. This is the place where decisions and choices in life are made (Deut. 21:14; 1 Chron. 22:19; Mark 8:35–38).

Mind. The mind is that invisible component of the brain comprising continual neurochemical and electromagnetic activity. Our mind has two sections, the conscious and subconscious mind. Persons can easily access and control their conscious mind but cannot easily access and control their subconscious mind. The subconscious mind is the person's database, where everything intentionally indulged in is stored together with the associated emotions and perceptions. It is an accumulation of the person's life experiences: good, bad, and indifferent. This is the faculty of intellect and involves the processing of and responding to the information and stimuli from the environment gathered by the five senses in the form of images, various forms of communication, thoughts, imaginations, and ideas to accumulate knowledge, understanding, and wisdom (Ezek. 24:25; Prov. 3:21–22; 19:2; Ps. 139:14–18).

Emotions. This faculty may be divided into three categories: affections, desires, and feelings and sensing.

1. *Affections.* this disposition is a fondness or tender feeling toward someone or something (Deut. 6:5; 1 Sam. 18:1; Luke 1:46).

2. *Desires.* These longing or craving emotions are, in themselves, neutral. Their moral is determined by the object of their attraction (Deut. 14:26; Ps. 84:2; Isa. 26:9).

3. *Feelings and sensing.* This is the storage of sensing impressions received from the five senses of the body (Luke 2:35; Job 19:2; Ps. 42:5; Matt. 26:38).

Body of Man

This physical element, which houses the spirit and soul of man, is what people see in the mirror. It provides man world-consciousness; medical science, biology, and hygiene provide much information regarding the nature and functions of our body. The Bible teaches that God designed man's body to be governed by their spirit, wherein dwells the righteousness and wisdom of God through Christ Jesus for every born-again believer (John 3:16–17; 10:10; Rom. 8:9–11). Unsaved persons are governed by their carnal minds and are subject to the promptings of the flesh (Rom. 8:5–8; 7:18–21).

Male and Female Man

The omniscient God created the race of man with the ability to reproduce after their kind. It is important to record at this point that God's order for procreation was set forth in the Garden of Eden experience.

> The Lord God said it was not good that the man should be alone, I will make him a help meet for him…And the Lord God caused a deep sleep to fall upon Adam, and he slept, and He took one of his ribs, and closed the flesh instead thereof. And the rib which the Lord God had taken from man, made He a woman and brought her unto the man. (Gen. 2:18, 21–22)

God the Creator and Lawgiver performed the first marriage ceremony Himself when He introduced female Adam to male Adam, for He named them both Adam (Gen. 5:2). Accordingly, marriage is a covenant between a man and a woman before the presence and person of God (or His representative), who alone can unite two souls (Malachi 2:14–16). Medical science informs us that the rib God used to make Eve had Adam's DNA or identity; no wonder God called them both Adam. By so doing, He was conveying His plan for them to have one mindset, a collective set of objectives and a consensus on all things. By conducting this ceremony, God established the first and most important institution in human society, the family. Like all other institutions, the family is equipped with a structure, a hierarchy of authority with corresponding responsibilities, facilitating order, growth, and development. Noteworthy is the fact that each member of the family is accountable to someone, for with responsibility and authority comes accountability. The husband and head of household, where husbands are absent, are accountable to God (Mal. 2:14–16; Ps. 127). God ordained for sexual intercourse to be the pleasurable experience of two responsible adults, a man and a woman expressing their love for each other by freely giving themselves without restraint. This level of relationship creates the nurturing, caring, psychological and emotional environment appropriate for the raising of children in the fear and admonition of the counsel of God.

God created mankind male and female, the male man possessing male reproductive anatomy and the female man possessing female reproductive anatomy. The male reproductive system consists of several sex organs that play a role in the reproduction of mankind. These organs are located on the outside of the male body and within the pelvis. The main male sex organs are the penis and the testicles, which produce semen and sperm. The female reproductive system consists of the internal and external sex organs that function in the reproduction of offspring. The female reproductive system is immature at birth and develops to maturity at puberty to gain the ability to produce gametes and carry a fetus to full term. The internal sex organs of the female are the vagina, uterus, fallopian tubes, and the ovaries. The vagina permits sexual intercourse and childbirth and is connected to the uterus at the cervix. The uterus, or womb, accommodates the embryo, which develops into the fetus.[15]

---

15   *Wikipedia,* male and female reproductive systems.

The prophetic word of God provides several characteristics of the last days, the era preceding the second advent of Christ. I wish to refer to two of these texts since they bear relevance to this matter.

> This know also, that in the last days perilous times shall come. For men shall be lovers of their own selves, covetous, boasters, proud, blasphemers, disobedient to parents, unthankful, unholy, without natural affection, trucebreakers, false accusers, incontinent, fierce, despisers of those that are good, traitors, heady, highminded, lovers of pleasures more than lovers of God. (2 Tim. 3:1–4)

> For the wrath of God is revealed from heaven against all ungodliness and unrighteousness of men, who hold the truth in unrighteousness. Because that which may be known of God is manifest in them; for God has shown it unto them. For the invisible things of Him from the creation of the world are clearly seen, being understood by the things that are made, even His eternal power and Godhead; so that they are without excuse. Because that when they knew God, they glorified Him not as God, neither were thankful, but became vain in their imaginations, and their foolish heart was darkened. Professing themselves to be wise, they became fools... Wherefore God also gave them up to uncleanness through the lusts of their own hearts, to dishonor their own bodies between themselves...For this cause God gave them up unto vile affections; for even their women did change the natural use into that which is against nature. And likewise, also the men leaving the natural use of the woman, burned in their lust one toward another; men with men working that which is unseemly, and receiving in themselves that recompence of their

error which was meet. (Rom. 1:18–22, 24, 26–27)

The cultures of many nations today have undergone drastic gender changes, whereby people are permitted to legally change their gender identity from male to female and vice versa. In some cases, these persons undergo surgical procedures to permit them to engage in sexual intercourse.

God's expressed desire, "Be fruitful and multiply," was for man to reproduce after his kind within the loving and nurturing boundaries of marriage. His purposes for man are designed to lead him into a deeper relationship with Him, permitting mankind to access greater divine benefits and rewards (John 10:10; Heb. 11:6).

CHAPTER 5

GOD'S DISPENSATIONAL DEALINGS WITH MAN PART 1

Although God has one plan of salvation, He employed various ways of dealing with mankind over protracted periods. According to Dr. Thiessen, whose views I endorse, the scriptures indicate that these periods of preparation were necessary for three reasons.

> To disclose to man the true nature of sin and the depth of depravity to which he has fallen, to reveal to him his powerlessness to preserve or regain an adequate knowledge of God or to deliver himself from sin by philosophy and art, and to teach him that forgiveness and restoration are possible only on the grounds of a substitutionary sacrifice. History shows how imperfectly the world learned these lessons, yet a partial learning of them was necessary before God could introduce the Savior in person.[16]

The Lord installed man in a perfect environment in the Garden of Eden, in a state of innocence, which was terminated by the fall. The following dispensations God employed were conscience, human

16   Thiessen, *Lectures in Systematic Theology*, 202.

government, promises, law, and grace. Because this presentation deals with the eternal purposes of God for mankind, I will also examine God's dealings with man beyond the current dispensation, the dispensation of grace. The prophetic word of God indicates that the dispensations of judgment and the millennial kingdom will precede the emergence of the eternal state.

The Dispensation of Innocence

A dispensation is a probationary period wherein the race of man is tested by God in relation to His revealed will. Hence, the dispensation of innocence was that period from the creation of man to the fall, during which Adam and Eve were tested to determine the way they would exercise their free will, whether they would choose to obey the righteous commands of God or disobey by acting independent of God. The key word *innocence* describes the character of that period, when man was in a state of guiltlessness in relation to sin. During this time, Adam and Eve enjoyed the immediate presence of God in fellowship, when He came down to the Garden of Eden in the cool of day to commune with them (Gen. 3:8).

The scripture declares that God the Son created man, male and female, in His own image and after His likeness (Gen. 1:26– 27; Col. 1:16). He formed Adam and placed him in the Garden of Eden and assigned him the responsibility of manager of all His creation (Gen. 2:15). Adam was so attuned to the wisdom of God that he correctly named every animal God created according to their nature (Gen. 2:19). God later caused Adam to go into a deep sleep and used a rib from his chest to form his companion, Eve (Gen. 2:21–23). God later presented Eve to Adam, who promptly named her Eve and called her woman, but God named them both Adam (Gen. 5:2).

The main personalities or participants in the period of innocence were God the Father, God the Son, and God the Holy Spirit, Satan, Adam, Eve, and the serpent. Satan was not identified by name in the scriptures, but he used the body of the serpent to communicate with Eve, for snakes have no capacity for speech (Gen. 3:1–5). The Lord gave Adam and Eve liberty to partake of every fruit tree and herb-bearing seed, except for the tree of the "knowledge of good and evil" that was amid the garden. God told him that if he should partake of the fruit of that tree, he would surely die. The scriptures does not indicate who informed Eve of the commandment. Adam may have instructed Eve concerning the commandment, for in her dialogue with the serpent, she added the clause "neither shall ye touch it" (Gen. 3:3b). Satan, using the serpent, deceived Eve and persuaded her to partake of the fruit of the tree of the "knowledge of good and evil." She ate and gave to Adam, who likewise ate, disobeying the commandment of God (Gen. 3:6).

Satan lied to Eve, but Adam was aware that the choice before him was one of association; the choice involved breaking his association and relationship with God or his wife, Eve. Issues leading up to Adam's sin may be debated, such as whether he was present when the serpent deceived Eve or the thoughts or influences he considered before deciding to join Eve in disobeying God or whether they really understood the meaning of the term "to die." The scriptures indicate that Adam was present with Eve when she took the fruit (Gen. 3:6b). It is certain from the scriptures that Adam was vested with the power to subdue and expel Satan from the garden when he began to speak to Eve, but he stood by and did not intervene (Gen. 1:28).

Having observed the intimacy of the animals around the garden, Adam may have decided to yield to his physical appetite and impulses instead of his spiritual and soulish needs. Some scholars may assume that Adam was uncertain of the meaning of the term "death" expressed by God, but I am certain that Adam did not, at that time, lose his ability to correctly perceive the communication of God. The ability he used to correctly name the animals was his until he yielded to the temptation and sinned (Gen. 2:17). He chose to disobey God and, by so doing, brought sin into the world, thereby terminating the dispensation of innocence.

Adam's sin, which ended the dispensation, had severe consequences as God warned. The reader, therefore, needs to examine God's judgment to learn the consequences that act brought about in the universe. God's word is always true, for Adam and Eve immediately lost their righteous standing with God. The minute he sinned, they were changed morally, experiencing spiritual death, and lost a true knowledge and fellowship with God. Guilt and fear entered their hearts, and they became corrupt and sought to hide from the presence of God. In response to God's query, they began to lie, casting the blame on others. Even before pronouncing the judgments, God prophesied the deliverance of man from the fall via the seed of the woman who was deceived by Satan. "Her seed will bruise thy head and thou will bruise his heel" (Gen. 3:15).

In pronouncing judgment, God first judged Satan and the serpent, whose very structure and nature were transformed from a deerlike animal (cattle) to a crawling reptile (Gen. 3:14). Our desire has the potential of changing our identity, character, structure, our entire world, and our destiny. The serpent was enticed and allowed the devil to use his body, thereby submitting himself to the devil instead of Adam, as God had created him. It was wise, cunning, and inquisitive, ignoring warning signs and boundaries set for its protection like so many people, especially youths. The serpent was a swift four-footed hoofed animal like the deer, but after the curse in verse 14, it became what it is today, the snake. What a change! Isn't this the same experience we see today when we observe homosexuals, lesbians, prostitutes, drunkards, and criminals? These people were not always that way. They gave themselves to destructive desires, which, over a period, lured them out of their sane minds. The devil tempted and teased them with promises of pleasure, popularity, and money, among other attractions, and stole their very souls. As a man thinks in his heart, so is he. People need to master their thoughts, for they become their words. They need to master their words, for they become their actions or deeds. People need to master their actions, for they form their habits, and they need to master their habits, for they determine their destiny in life and eternity (Prov. 23:7).

Second, God judged the woman, increasing her sorrow in childbearing and assigning her desire to her husband, to whom she must be submitted (Gen. 3:16). He, thereafter, judged the earth, causing it to bring forth thorns and thistles, increasing the labor of man, and finally, He judged Adam, assigning him to labor all his days. "In the sweat of thy face thou shall eat bread till thou return unto the ground" (Gen. 3:18–19). Having disobeyed God, Adam and Eve's nature and disposition changed. They could no longer fellowship with God face-to-face. He cast them out of the Garden of Eden and placed cherubim and a flaming sword to prevent them from having access to the tree of life in the middle of the garden. Praise God, in the fullness of time, He sent forth His Son, the seed of the woman, to provide salvation so man can receive eternal life and fellowship with Him today (Gal. 4:4).

Dispensation of Conscience

This dispensation began at the fall of man and extended to the time of God's judgment by flood, covering a period of approximately 1,656 years.[17] God, the Lawgiver, activated the conscience of man to act as his agent to bear witness of His presence, righteous nature, and law (Gen. 3:23–24; Rom. 1:18–20). Cain, the murderer, lived and had children, who multiplied, accomplishing many human endeavors, namely, becoming skilled tent builders, herders of cattle, musicians skilled in the use of the harp and organ, while others were skilled metal workers of brass and iron (Gen. 4:17–22). Cain himself built a city and named it after his son Enoch. Adam and Eve bore another son; Eve rejoiced, thanking God for blessing her with a replacement for Abel, in whom God delighted. She named him Seth; he had a heart like his deceased brother, Abel, to seek after the Lord. The birth of his first son, Enos, so inspired Seth that he initiated the worship of God previously practiced by Abel, marking a revival of public worship, where people began to call on the name of the Lord (Gen. 4:25–26). The descendants of Seth displayed a righteous lifestyle for a period in their cities, but with the passing of time, their children intermarried with the descendants of Cain, and gradually, all piety disappeared from the race of man on earth. There was no seeking after God in the generations of man. Their conscience grew dull, and every imagination of the thoughts of their hearts was only evil continually.

> And it repented God that He had made man on the earth, and it grieved Him at His heart. And the Lord said I will destroy man whom I have created from the face of the earth; both man and beast and the creeping thing, and the fowls of the air; for it repented me that I have made them,

---

17 Jones, *Rose Book of Bible Charts, Maps and Timelines.*

But Noah found grace in the eyes of the Lord.
(Gen. 6:6–8)

Dispensation of Human Government

This dispensation commenced after the flood with Noah and his family, with whom God made a covenant that formed the basis of all human governments onto today. The eight provisions of this covenant God made with Noah and his sons were intended to govern human life and human government on earth after the flood.[18] God the Creator and Lawgiver is sovereign and never compromises with the wishes or demands of man. History reveals that God is always in control of every aspect of His universe. He sets the laws, and man is required to observe them or endure the consequences of their disobedience. The preamble to the covenant states, "But with thee I will establish my covenant; and thou shall come into the ark, thou and thy sons, thy wife and thy sons' wives with thee" (Gen. 6:18). It was God's plan to preserve the race of man and the animals through Noah and his family by the ark from

His judgment upon the earth. The provisions of the covenant are set out hereunder.

1. And the Lord smelled a sweet savor, and the Lord said in His heart, I will not again curse the ground any more for man's sake, for the imagination of man's heart is evil from his youth, neither will I again smite any more everything living as I have done. While the earth remain seedtime and harvest, and cold and heat, and summer and winter, and day and night shall not cease. (Gen. 8:21–22)

By this provision, God made nature very predictable; this predictability forms the basis of all modern science and investigation. The faithfulness of God to His promise has caused many scientists to ignore the fact that God has the prerogative to interrupt the course of nature whenever He chooses, as He has done several times in history to remind man that He is in control.

---

18   Ray Stedman, authentic Christianity, raystedman.org.

2.   And God blessed Noah and his sons and said unto them, be fruitful and multiply and replenish the earth. And the fear of you and the dread of you shall be upon every beast of the earth, and upon every fowl of the air, upon all that move upon the earth, and upon all the fishes of the sea, into your hand are they delivered. (Gen. 9:1–2)

This is the reason animals, in general, fear human beings; some have been domesticated by training, but there is an instinctive dread of mankind in the animal kingdom. There are some animals that man have never been able to tame; the news media frequently share stories of pet animals—dogs, snakes, tigers, lions, among others—killing their owners. Before the fall of man, Adam and Eve and all the animals dwelled together in harmony; however, the fall brought about drastic changes in man's nature. The image and likeness of God in mankind became marred by the plague of sin.

3.   Every moving thing that lives shall be meat for you, even as the green herb, have I given you all things. (Gen. 9:3)

Ray Stedman, author of *Authentic Christianity*, made some poignant observations in this regard, with which I concur. Mankind seems to be the most dependent animal; they are alive because other animals and plants have died on their behalf. Man having added animals to their menu, the Lord made an important requirement.

4.   But flesh with the life thereof, which is the blood thereof, shall ye not eat. And surely your blood of your lives will I require, at the hand of every beast will I require it, and at the hand of man; at the hand of every man's brother will I require the life of man. (Gen. 9:4–5)

God established that the life of man is very sacred; He placed the life of all living things in the blood, and it belongs to Him alone. He seeks to maintain His sovereignty over every form of life; He is the source, creator, and sustainer of all life and will avenge anyone who violates His righteous laws by taking the life of another person. "Vengeance is mine saith the Lord" (Rom. 12:19b). Knowing the hearts of men, the Lord warns against seeking revenge. He has set governments to administer justice in those cases where a crime has been committed

(Rom. 13:4). Yes, this passage of scripture can correctly be used as a basis for capital punishment in federal and state legal systems. Ray Stedman contends that God's requirement applies not only to men but also for animals' life to be taken if they caused the death of an individual or child. This establishes the life of mankind to be off limits for everyone, except for governments, who operate as His agents in the execution of justice (Gen. 9:5–6). I endorse his view that the aforementioned text establishes God's exclusive right to the life of every man, even the criminal, and no one is permitted to take justice into their own hands.

5.   Whosoever shed man's blood, by man shall his blood be shed: for in the image of God made He man. (Gen. 9:6)

I endorse the views of Stedman, who states that God, unlike humans, sees the race of man as one vast body of humanity, a brotherhood of one flesh, past, present, and future. God requires of the race of man a price for the shed blood of every individual, not only the guilty party. Murder and manslaughter will be avenged against the entire race of mankind. The price may be extracted in a variety of ways: accidents, more violence, natural disasters. God established the principle that violence begets violence. Bloodshed begets more bloodshed—a cycle man can resolve only by recognizing their helplessness and seeking divine intervention (Jer. 9:24).

6.   And you be fruitful and multiply, bring forth abundantly in the earth and multiply therein. (Gen. 9:7)

This clause outlines God's desire for man to reproduce after his kind and fill, dress, and keep the earth. The character of man is revealed in his dealings with other persons; in isolation, people may seek to embrace the illusion of their independence from God, but a dense population brings to light our need for God, who alone can help people deal with the challenges of life in these last days.

7.   And God spoke unto Noah and to his sons with him saying, behold I establish my covenant with you and your seed after you. And with every living creature that is with you, of the fowl, of the cattle, and of every beast of the earth with you, from all that go out of the ark, to every beast of the earth. And I will establish my covenant with you; neither shall all

flesh be cut off anymore by the waters of a flood; neither shall there anymore be a flood to destroy the earth. (Gen. 9:8–11)

This promise God made to Noah and his family has been kept, for God is always faithful to His Word. The promise addresses the method of God's judgment and clearly does not indicate that God will not bring judgment upon the race of man again. The New Testament informs readers that this time, God will judge by fire instead of water. "It is appointed unto men once to die and after this the judgment" (Heb. 9:27). "But the heavens and the earth which are now, by the same word are kept in store, reserved unto fire against the day of judgment and perdition of ungodly men" (2 Peter 3:7).

8.   And God said this is the token of the covenant which I make between me and you and every living creature that is with you for perpetual generations. I do set my bow in the cloud, and it shall be for a token of a covenant between me and the earth. And it shall come to pass when I bring a cloud over the earth, that the bow shall be seen in the cloud; And I will remember my covenant, which is between me and you and every living creature of all flesh; and the waters shall no more become a flood to destroy all flesh. And the bow shall be in the cloud; and I will look upon it, that I may remember the everlasting covenant between God and every living creature of all flesh that is upon the earth. (Gen. 9:12–16).

This final clause of the covenant God made with Noah and his family deals with the sign God established in a place visible to all—in the skies, amid the threatening clouds, a glorious multicolored bow affirming that He will never again bring a universal flood to destroy the earth. The rainbow is a testimony that God is always faithful to His Word. He exalts it above His name to perform it. Hence, the Word of God is faithful and true. For me, it is a sign of the love, grace, and mercy of our sovereign God. I agree with Stedman that God is speaking to mankind via each of the preceding clauses of the covenant: the reliability of nature, the instinctive fear of man among animals, the meals people partake of daily, the violence and injustices in society.

These situations reflect God's grace and mercy on one hand and mankind's inability to overcome the cycle of despair produced by the plague of sin on the other.

Like Adam, Noah was directed to govern for God by instituting just and holy laws. However, the generations after him sought to establish a name for themselves and built a tower, the Tower of Babel, giving glory and praise to themselves instead of God. Accordingly, God intervened and broke their communication by confounding their speech. This was the initial establishment of different languages and a federation of nations all over the earth. The corrupt nature of man's heart led them to continue their pursuit of evil; the imaginations and thoughts of their hearts were evil continually rather than seeking after the face of God their Creator (Gen. 8:21).

The Dispensation of Promise

This dispensation began with God's call of Abram out of the land of the Chaldees and into a covenant relationship with Him, recorded in Genesis 12 and 15. The dispensation ended with God's miraculous deliverance of the children of Israel from the Egyptian bondage following His final plague judgment upon Egypt, the death of the firstborn (Exod. 11–12). Abram's father, Terah, migrated his family from Ur of the Chaldees to the land of Canaan (Gen. 11:31). The Lord, however, spoke to Abram while they were in transit and made several promises to him.

> And I will make of thee a great nation, and I will
> bless thee, and make thy name great; and thou
> shall be a blessing. And I will bless them that
> bless thee and curse them that curse thee; and
> in thee shall all families of the earth be blessed.
> (Gen. 12:2–3)

In each dispensation so far, God chose one family to function as His representative and witness to the world of His identity, righteous nature, and requirement for life, His love, grace, and mercy. Abram became the sole witness of the True and Living God in an idolatrous world; he had to change his belief system and values to conform to God's holy requirements. Twenty-five years elapsed between the promise God made to Abram in Genesis 12 and Sarah's conception with Isaac, the son of promise. Abram's wife, Sarai, became impatient and decided to give her maid Hagar to Abram for wife, as the custom was in those days. Abram made the same mistake Adam made in acting on his wife's ungodly advice and took Hagar as his wife; the union brought forth Ishmael, the father of the Arab nations.

When he first received the promise from God, Abram was seventy-five years old. God appeared again unto him in a vision when he was ninety-nine years old and rehearsed the promise. This time, He said,

> I am the Almighty God, walk before me and be thou perfect. And I will make my covenant between me and thee and will multiply thee exceedingly....And I will give unto thee and to thy seed after thee, the land wherein thou art a stranger, all the land of Canaan, for an everlasting possession; and I will be their God. (Gen. 17:1b–2)

God tested the faith of Abram and Sarai for the twenty-five years they waited. When the Lord appeared to Abram the third time and announced that his wife, Sarai, would conceive and bear him a son, who would be the son of promise, he believed and it was accounted unto him for righteousness (Gen. 17:15–19). The Lord gave Abraham several commandments with promises as outlined hereunder.

1. Walk thou before me, and be thou perfect, and I will make my covenant between me and thee, and will multiply thee exceedingly. (Gen. 17:1b–2)

2. Neither shall thy name any more be called Abram, but thy name shall be called Abraham, for a Father of many nations have I made thee. (Gen. 17:5)

3. Every child among you shall be circumcised; and you shall circumcise the flesh of your foreskin, and it shall be a token of the covenant betwixt me and you. (Gen. 17:10b–11)

4.   And he that is eight days old shall be circumcised among you, every man child in your generation, he that is born in the house, or bought with money of any stranger which is not of thy seed. (Gen. 17:12)

5.   He that is born in thy house and he that is bought with thy money must needs be circumcised, and my covenant shall be in your flesh for an everlasting covenant, and the uncircumcised man-child whose flesh of his foreskin is not circumcised, that soul shall be cut off from his people; he has broken my covenant. (Gen. 17:13–14)

The Lord rehearsed the foregoing promises to Isaac (Gen. 26:1–5) and Jacob (Gen. 28:12–16) as promised. With the passing of time, Abraham's descendants grew and multiplied greatly in the wilderness of Paran (Ishmael's seed) and the land of Canaan (Isaac's seed). I now wish to address the origin of the Jewish race, the nation of Israel. As Jacob returned to Canaan with his family and their possessions, he was engrossed with fear of his brother Esau's retaliation, although the Lord made several efforts to assure him that He was with him and will protect him (Gen. 32:7, 11). The Lord sent angels to console Jacob at a place he called Mahanaim (Gen. 32:1–2). However, Jacob was still very fearful of Esau's retaliation for coveting his birthright and blessing. So the Lord decided to console him in person. Being alone, Jacob assumed that the person who approached him late that night meant to harm him, so he began to fight for his life. Jacob later realized that the person he was fighting had no desire to harm him; he discerned that he was wrestling with the Lord God. Realizing the danger of wrestling with God, Jacob demanded a blessing from the Lord. In response, the Lord announced to him, "Thy name shall be called no more Jacob, but Israel, for as a prince hast thou power with God and with men, and hast prevailed" (Gen. 32:28).

The omniscient God used the strife between Joseph, one of Jacob's youngest sons, and his elder brothers to send Joseph to Egypt, where he continued to prepare him through much suffering for the elevated destiny He had for him, that of becoming Prime Minister of Egypt and gaining the favor of Pharaoh the king. Joseph, a great man of God, interpreted two dreams the king had and found great favor with

Pharaoh, who chose him to execute the plan he proposed to deal with the great famine that was imminent in the region (Gen. 41).

God revealed to Pharaoh via two dreams what was about to occur in that part of the world. After seven years of bountiful harvests of food crops, the nations would experience seven years of grievous famine. The famine ravished the entire region of countries, including Canaan, where Jacob's family dwelt. Joseph's brothers travelled to Egypt to buy food but did not recognize him. Joseph remembered two dreams he had as a lad in Canaan and realized that God was using him to make provision not only for his family but for the people of Egypt and the surrounding nations of the region. Being endowed with the wisdom of God, Joseph orchestrated an intriguing plan to reveal himself to his brothers and to finally bring his father, Jacob, and his entire family to Egypt to live in comfort. Pharaoh welcomed Joseph's family to Egypt and gave approval for them to occupy Goshen, where some of the best pastures in Egypt were located.

After the death of Pharaoh, the friend of Joseph, a new king who had no respect for the service of Joseph to the nation of Egypt, ascended to the kingdom. The new king was afraid of the children of Israel, who multiplied greatly in the land, and sought to oppress them, removing the benefits they enjoyed for thirty years. God revealed to Abraham in a vision that his seed would be besieged and afflicted in a strange land for four hundred years but would be delivered after four generations with great wealth (Gen. 15:13–16). As promised, the Lord raised up Moses, an offspring of Jacob, who was miraculously raised in Pharaoh's palace, to deliver the children of Israel. The Lord prepared Moses and his brother, Aaron, to appear before the new Pharaoh.

Egypt was an idolatrous nation where the people worshipped about five hundred false gods. The Lord hardened the heart of the king and prolonged his negotiations with Moses for the release of the children of Israel from their servitude. As Moses appealed to the king, the burdens and oppression of the people of Israel were increased. God inflicted the nation of Egypt with ten plagues to demonstrate His superiority to their false gods. There were plagues of water turning to blood, frogs infestation of the nation, lice or gnats infestation of the land, fly infestation of the nation, a livestock-killing plague, a plague of boils on men and animals, a plague of hail that killed men and animals, a plague of locusts, which devoured all vegetation in the land, thick darkness covering the nation for three days, and finally, the death of every firstborn man and beast. Goshen was not affected because the Lord protected the children of Israel from the plagues that inflicted the land of Egypt.

The Lord commanded Moses and Aaron to instruct the children of Israel to prepare the Passover feast.

> In the tenth day of the month of Abib, take every man a lamb, according to the house of their fathers, a lamb for a house and if the household be too little for the lamb, let him and his neighbor next unto his house take it according to the number of the souls, every man according to his eating shall make your count for the lamb. Your lamb shall be without blemish, a male of the first year; you shall take it out from the sheep or goats, and you shall keep it up until the fourteenth day of the same month; and the whole congregation of Israel shall kill it in the evening. And they shall take of the blood and strike it on the two side posts and on the upper door post of the houses, wherein they shall eat it. And they shall eat the flesh in that night, roast with fire and unleavened bread and with bitter herbs they shall eat it. Eat not of it raw, nor sodden at all with water, but roast with fire, his head with his legs and with the purtenance thereof. And you shall let nothing of it remain until the morning; and that which remain of it until the morning you shall burn with fire. And thus, shall you eat it; with your loins girded; your shoes on your feet and your staff in your hand and you shall eat it in haste; it is the Lord's Passover. For I will pass through the land of Egypt this night and will smite all the firstborn in the land of Egypt, both man and

> beast; and against all the gods of Egypt I will
> execute judgment; I am the Lord. And the blood
> shall be to you for a token upon the houses where
> you are and when I see the blood, I will pass
> over you and the plague shall not be upon you
> to destroy you when I smite the land of Egypt.
> (Exod. 12:3–13)

The might and supernatural power of the God of Israel brought great fear on the hearts of all the inhabitants of Egypt, including the king, who, mourning the death of his son, hastily instructed Moses to gather the children of Israel and leave. Shortly before the nation was afflicted with the final plague, the Lord instructed the children of Israel to ask their Egyptian neighbors and those that were among them for gold, silver, and precious ornaments and clothing and give them to their children (Exod. 3:21–22; 12:36). Accordingly, Moses and the children of Israel, numbering about two million, including six hundred thousand able-bodied men besides women and children, departed Egypt and travelled toward the wilderness of the Red Sea (Exod. 12:37).

The children of Israel travelled from Succoth along the way of the wilderness of the Red Sea and set camp at Etham on the first day and Migdol by the Red Sea on the second day. The miraculous presence of God led them by a pillar of cloud during the day and by a pillar of fire at night, providing light and comfort. God notified Moses that He would cause Pharaoh to have a change of heart and pursue them to return them to servitude but would defeat the king and his army so the nations would know that He, the God of Israel, is Lord (Exod. 14:4). The sight of the army of Egypt in pursuit caused the children of Israel to be afraid and murmur against Moses and Aaron. Israel was surrounded by mountains on both sides, the Red Sea before them, and Pharaoh's army behind them. To the people of Israel, the situation appeared hopeless, but God had a miraculous plan for their deliverance.

He commanded Moses to stretch forth his rod over the waters of the Red Sea, and the waters rolled back on either side, revealing a path of dry land for the people to cross to the other side (Exod. 14:15–18). Moreover, the angel of the Lord, in the form of the pillar of cloud and fire that led the children of Israel, removed from before them and stood behind them, protecting them from Pharaoh and his army. The Lord caused the seabed that was dry for Israel to become soggy for the Egyptians, so their chariot wheels began to break, and fear came upon them, for they cried, "Let us flee from the face of Israel, for the Lord fights for them against us" (Exod. 14:25b). After the children of Israel crossed over the Red Sea to the other side, the Lord instructed Moses to stretch his hand over the sea, and it returned to its full strength, so the waters overcame the army of Egyptians. The chariots, the horsemen, and all the host of Pharaoh who pursued Israel into the Red Sea, they all died in the sea (Exod. 14:27–28).

So the Lord honored the prophetic word He spoke unto Abraham concerning His deliverance of his seed from the yoke of bondage in Egypt and affirmed the authority of His servants Moses and Aaron, whom He chose to lead the children of Israel (Gen. 15:13–1):

> And Israel saw that great work which the Lord
> did upon the Egyptians: and the people feared
> the Lord and believed the Lord and His servant
> Moses. Then sang Moses and the children of
> Israel...the Lord is my strength and song, and
> He is become my salvation: He is my God, and
> I will prepare Him a habitation; my father's God
> and I will exalt Him. The Lord is a man of war;
> the Lord is His name. (Exod. 14:31–15:1–3)

It is important to note that like in the dispensation of human government, where God instituted laws for the entire race of man via Noah and his sons, so it is in the dispensations of promise and law as God's plan was to set the seed of Abraham, Isaac, and Jacob as a godly pattern and blessing to all the nations of the world.

CHAPTER 6

GOD'S DISPENSATIONAL DEALINGS WITH MAN PART 2

The Dispensation of Law

This dispensation began with the deliverance of the two million descendants of Jacob from the Egyptian bondage to serve the God of their fathers—Abraham, Isaac, and Jacob—in the wilderness of Sinai (Exod. 7:16; 19:1). God called Moses up unto Him in Mount Sinai and instructed him to say to the people,

> You have seen what I did unto the Egyptians and how I bare you on eagles wings and brought you unto myself. Now therefore, if you will obey my voice indeed, and keep my covenant, then you shall be a peculiar treasure unto me above all people, for all the earth is mine. And you shall be unto me a kingdom of priests, and a holy nation. (Exod. 19:4–6a)

Moses gathered the elders of the people together and did as God instructed him, and the people agreed to do all that the Lord requested (Exod. 19:8). The Lord then instructed Moses to sanctify the people and prepare them to stand before Him on the third day, when He would descend on the mountain to speak to them in person. Boundaries were set so that no man or animal could come near the mountain to touch it, for they would die. At the appointed time, the trumpets of God sounded loud and long as the Lord God descended in fire on the top of Mount Sinai, which shook with great thunders and lightning. When he gathered with the people as the Lord instructed, Moses spoke, and God answered from the mount with a voice and called him up unto the mountain for further instructions.

The children of Israel became fearful of the awesome presence of God, with the thunder, the lightning, the sounds of the trumpets, and the shaking of the smoking mountain. They then requested that Moses speak to God and convey His words to them, because they feared personal encounters with the Lord, lest they die. In response, Moses exhorted the people, "Fear not for God is come to prove you, and that His fear may be before your faces, that you sin not" (Exod. 20:20). The people moved and stood afar off, but Moses drew near to the thick darkness where the Lord was, and God spoke, commanding him to speak to the people all the words of the covenant laws governing their lifestyle, worship, family relationships, among others (Exod. 20–23). Emphasizing the fact that He, unlike the gods of other nations, is a living God, the Lord said, "You have seen that I have talked with you from heaven" (Exod. 20:22). "Moses told the people all the words and judgments of the Lord and all the people answered with one voice and said all the words which the Lord hath said will we do" (Exod. 24:3).

> And Moses wrote all the words of the Lord and rose early in the morning and built an altar under the hill, and twelve pillars according to the twelve tribes of Israel. And he sent young men of the children of Israel, which offered burnt offerings, and sacrificed peace offerings of oxen unto the Lord. And Moses took half of the blood and put it in basons; and half of the blood he sprinkled on the altar. And he took the book of the covenant and read in the audience of the people; and they said all that the Lord hath said will we do and be obedient. And Moses took the blood and sprinkled it on the people and said behold

the blood of the covenant, which the Lord hath made with you concerning all these words. (Exod. 24:4–8)

The Lord called Moses, Aaron, Nadab, Abihu, the sons of Aaron, and seventy of the elders of Israel unto Himself in the mountain to worship. They worshiped the Lord from a distance and had fellowship eating and drinking in the presence of God (Exod. 24:10–11). The Lord then called Moses alone to the top of the mountain to receive tablets of stone containing laws and commandments for the nation of Israel. The elders returned to the congregation of Israel, but Moses and Joshua, his minister, went up to meet with the Lord on Mount Sanai and communed with God for forty days (Exod. 24:12–18). Thereafter, the Lord gave Moses instructions to request the children of Israel to bring unto him an offering willingly to be used to build a sanctuary for Him to dwell among them. The offerings included gold, silver, brass, fine linen in purple, blue, and scarlet hues, goats hair and ram skins dyed red, badgers skins, shittimwood, oil for light, spices for anointing oil and for sweet incense, onyx stones, and stones to be set in the ephod and in the breastplate. The Lord gave detailed instructions on the building of the tabernacle with its divisions, all the furniture required for the various functions of the priests, the attire of the priests, and the establishment of the priesthood and Levites with their orders and functions.

The tabernacle was a moveable tent having three compartments: the outer court, where the people brought their sacrifices to the priests and where the bronze altar and bronze laver were located; the inner court, or the holy place, where the golden lampstand, incense altar, and the table with showbread were located; and the most holy place, where the Ark of the Covenant was located. God gave the law and ordinances to the children of Israel to reveal to them His standard of righteousness and their sinful nature, to cause them to acknowledge their inability to please Him in their own strength, and to point them to Christ their Messiah and Redeemer (Rom. 3:20).

After Moses and the children of Israel completed the building and erection of the tabernacle with all its furnishings and the priests' and Levites' garments were completed according to the instructions of the Lord, Moses put the Ark of the Covenant in the most holy place. The showbread was placed on the table in the holy place. The candles on the golden lampstand were lit, and he burnt sweet incense on the golden altar. He offered burnt offerings and meat offerings in the tent of the congregation, the outer court, as the Lord commanded. The laver bowl with water to wash was placed between the altar and the tent of the congregation. Moses, Aaron, and his sons then entered the outer courts and washed their hands and feet as they approached the altar as the Lord commanded. Having completed all the work, Moses then hung the court gate in place, and a cloud covered the tent of the congregation, and the glory of the Lord filled the tabernacle. The children of Israel abode in their place until the cloud was lifted from over the tabernacle, then they proceeded on their daily journey.

Israel came out of bondage with great material wealth, but with a slave mentality, they rebelled against Moses and his successor, Joshua, and provoked the Lord to the extent that He caused the generation that left Egypt to die in the wilderness, except for Joshua and Caleb. God was very patient with the people, but they had no desire to seek after the purposes and will of God and continuously provoked the Lord to anger by their disobedience. Israel's journey from Egypt to Canaan was not a logistical journey; it was a journey in character, integrity, and relationship with God. This trip that took forty years may have been completed in three weeks, but God was the Guide of His people and did not allow them to go further than they could follow His commandments. The covenant He made with their forefathers required their obedience for its fulfillment.

The children of Israel entered the Promised Land, Canaan, under the leadership of Joshua but continued their cycle of disobedience, which often led to oppression by other nations. God used fifteen judges to deliver them from oppression, but after a time of peace, they returned to their former ways, worshipping false gods. During the ministry of Samuel, who served as a prophet and judge, the people demanded a king like other nations. The Lord reluctantly granted their request with the appointment of King Saul, who was replaced by king David after forty years because he disobeyed the instructions of God. The lineage of kings in Israel mostly continued to disobey the will of God given them by God's messengers, the prophets, who they persecuted and, in some, instances killed. I endorse the views expressed below.

> God never expected perfection, if He did, He would not have provided the sacrificial system as a way for man to say, yes I have sinned; here is a symbol of my need for forgiveness and atonement. The blood of bulls and goats could not take away sins, they were a symbol pointing to the One whose blood alone could take away sins (Heb. 9:11–14; 10:3–10).[19]

The dispensation of law was terminated with the crucifixion of Jesus the Messiah on the cross of Calvary and signified by the rending of the veil of the temple in Jerusalem from top to bottom by the Holy Ghost. God decided to introduce a new era in His dealings with the race of man, the dispensation of grace, which continues at present. However, God has not completed His transactions with the seed of Abraham, Isaac, and Jacob. He will resume and fulfill all the covenant promises He made to the forefathers of Israel when He acts to establish His millennial kingdom in Jerusalem.

The Dispensation of Grace

This dispensation began with the resurrection of Jesus Christ from death and affirmed by the birth of the church on the day of Pentecost, when the one hundred and twenty believers were filled with the Holy Ghost and power from on High, as promised by the Lord.

> And behold I send the promise of my Father upon you, but tarry ye in the city of Jerusalem until ye be endued with power from on high. (Luke 24:49)

> But you shall receive power after that the Holy Ghost is come upon you, and you shall be witnesses unto me both in Jerusalem and in all Judea and in Samaria and onto the uttermost part of the earth. (Acts 1:8)

---

19   Compellingtruth.org/seven-dispensations.

The dispensation of grace is also referred to as the church age, which theologians agree will end with the rapture of the church, the body of Christ (1 Cor. 15:50–54; 1 Thess. 4:13–17). Jesus, God's foreordained lamb who was slain before the foundations of the world was laid, provided atonement for the entire race of man, Jews and Gentiles alike (Rev. 13:8b). Jesus bore the cumulative sin of the world, embracing every generation of mankind on the cross of Calvary. This gift of redemption provided by God through the atoning work of Jesus is granted only to those persons who, like Abraham, receives the invitation of the gospel by faith evidenced by the surrender of their life to Christ. God created man with the volition of free will and will never violate the will of any individual.

> Whosoever believeth in Christ, the Son of God, shall not perish but have everlasting life, for he that hath the Son hath life but he that hath not the Son of God hath not life. (John 3:16; 1 John 5:12)

The term "objective salvation" is used to refer to what God did to provide man's redemption. God repeated His Abrahamic covenant promises to Isaac and Jacob and gave similar promises to the church, Abraham's seed by faith. "But you are a chosen generation, a royal priesthood, an holy nation, a peculiar people; that you should show forth the praises of Him who hath called you out of darkness into His marvelous light" (1 Peter 2:9). Like the promise of blessing to all nations of the world via Abraham's seed, God commanded the church to spread the gospel of Christ to all nations (Matt. 28:19–20; Acts 1:8). God has been using the body of Christ, members of the church, to propagate the gospel to all the nations of the world.

I will now identify some differences between the dispensations of law and grace. First, they possess independent and complete systems of divine government. The Law of Moses was applicable only to the nation of Israel, a people God separated unto Himself. Man's failure to meet the righteous demands of God was forcefully revealed by the law, driving them to seek after God. The Law of Moses covered every aspect of Israel's life but was terminated by the death of Christ on the cross and signified by the divine rending of the veil of the temple (Matt. 27:51).

The present age of grace, like the Law of Moses, is not applicable to all men on the earth; it is an invitation to a peculiar people on earth, who, by faith, believe the gospel and yield their lives to Christ. God dealt very graciously with the race of man from Adam until Moses; Christ's sacrificial death was a necessary foundation for the full revelation of God's plan of grace. God's focus here is the individual believer; Jew and Gentile alike become new creatures in Christ, born again from heaven by the Holy Spirit (2 Cor. 5:17).

Second is the sequence of the divine blessing and the human obligation. By illustration, the law states, "If you do good works, I will bless you," while grace states, "I have blessed and equipped you, to do good works." The law begins by prescribing the meritorious work man must perform to receive the blessing of God, but grace informs man of the divine blessing God has bestowed, enabling the believer to perform good works (Deut. 28:1–68; 1 Cor. 2:9–16; Eph. 2:10).

Third and last, there are different degrees of difficulty and divine enablement. The standard of life required in the three dispensations and the divine enablement varies vastly. In the era of the Law of Moses, the standard of life required was unattainable by man, except for the Lord Jesus; that required under the kingdom era will be more advanced and intense legally than that of the law of Moses. There was no divine enablement in the era of the Law of Moses, but there will be three levels of divine enablement in the kingdom age, namely, the creation will be purified and delivered from bondage and corruption, Satan will be bound and cast into the bottomless pit, and the Lord will put His laws into the minds of the people and write them in their hearts and pour out His Spirit upon all flesh (Joel 2:28–32). The standard of life required in the present age of grace is beyond the standards outlined above for the two eras of law, for it is the requirement for citizens of heaven and attainable only by believers governed by the person of the Holy Spirit (Heb. 8:7–12; Rom. 8:9–14; Eph. 2:10).

The proclamation of the work of God was portrayed using different terms by different messengers; the apostles identified Jesus as the Christ (Acts 5:42), the Promise of the fathers (Acts 13:32). Luke used many other verses to demonstrate that Jesus was the focus of the apostles' preaching and teaching. Paul and Barnabas portrayed the gospel as

God's invitation to turn the Gentiles from worthless things, such as idols, to the Living God, who created the heavens, the earth, the sea, and everything within them. Luke presents the person and works of Jesus as the center of the gospel; the believer in Christ receives forgiveness of sins and the gift of eternal life, thereby establishing relationship with God the Father. He summarized the apostles' witness as follows.

> That Word, I say you know which was published throughout all Judea and began from Galilee after the baptism which John preached; how God anointed Jesus of Nazareth with the Holy Ghost and with power; who went about doing good and healing all that were oppressed of the devil; for God was with Him. And we are witnesses of all things which He did both in the land of the Jews and in Jerusalem, whom they slew and hanged on a tree. And He commanded us to preach unto the people, and to testify that it is He, which was ordained of God to be the Judge of the quick and dead. To Him give all the prophets witness, that through His Name whosoever believeth in Him shall receive remission of sins. (Acts 10:37–39; 42–43)

The gospel was proclaimed to all people in their locations. Jesus and the apostles preached in the Jewish synagogues on the Sabbath, in public settings in towns and villages. Sometimes Jesus used a boat on the seashore to address the people. The message of salvation conveyed the foretold promise to both Jews and Gentiles. In his introduction, Luke referred to Zachariah's prophecy that Jesus was the "horn" in the house of King David, a light shining on those who sat in darkness and death (Luke 1:69; 78–79; Isa. 42:6; 49:9). The universality and expansion of the gospel message was highlighted in the dramatic vision the Lord gave to Peter regarding the work of the Holy Spirit in the household of Cornelius. "What God has cleansed, call not thou common. This was done thrice" (Acts 10:15–16). Peter, in his message to Cornelius's household, gave assurance that salvation was available to all people from all nations, Jews and Gentiles.

Luke recorded many details on the expansion of the gospel to the Gentiles, the poor, sinners, and outcasts. The Jews as a nation rejected Christ as their Messiah, but He was gladly embraced by the Gentiles. A Gentile centurion exhibited such faith in Christ as the Son of God that Jesus remarked, "I have not found so great faith, no not in Israel" (Luke 7:9b). Jesus ministered in Samaria; He also shared a parable of the Good Samaritan, who exhibited the love of God to a wounded stranger in need while several Jews refused to help. Jesus healed ten lepers, but only one, a Samaritan, returned to Jesus to worship and thank Him. Luke, the writer of the Acts of the Apostles, demonstrated God's personal involvement in proclaiming the gospel to the Gentile nations. The Lord's encounter with Saul on the road to Damascus and his later commission charging him to bear His name before the Gentiles and "open their eyes and turn them from darkness to light and from the power of Satan unto God, that they may receive forgiveness of sins and an inheritance among them that are sanctified by faith demonstrates God's intent to reach the Gentile nations with the gospel" (Acts 26:18). Jesus's concern for the poor and outcasts was exhibited in the attention He gave to the generous gift of the widow who gave her last mite as an offering to the Lord and, secondly, His commitment to dine with Zacchaeus the tax collector, who the religious sects regarded as an outcast. Jesus gladly communed with the common people and was accused by the religious sects of communing with sinners.

In his writing of the Gospel of Luke and the Acts of the Apostles, Luke not only recorded the life and ministry of Jesus but revealed who He was. We learn that Jesus was the foreordained Lamb of God (sinless and spotless), born of a virgin (seed of the woman, not the seed of man), Son of God (born of the Holy Ghost), Horn of King David (lineage of Abraham and King David), Messiah, Innocent Sufferer, who bore our sins and iniquities on the cross of Calvary, and the Compassionate Son of Man, who forgave His enemies and left vindication in the hands of His Father in heaven.

Subjective salvation deals with the personal application or reception of God's salvation—that is, the response God requires of every individual who desires the benefits of redemption. It is important to note that although Jesus bore the cumulative sin of humans on the cross of Calvary, the gift of salvation must be claimed individually; everyone must choose who they will serve in life. God requires every soul to give an account for the opportunity He provides them to hear and respond to the gospel of His saving grace, in the sacrifice of His only begotten Son (Acts, 4:12; John 3:16–17). Luke indicates that there is only one favorable response to God's invitation, a total surrender to the claims of Christ. This response of faith is the act of man's will, whereby they acknowledge their sinful and corrupt nature, which only Christ alone can cure. The Holy Spirit, who opens the eyes of the person's understanding, convicts them of sin, righteousness and judgment wooing them to true repentance (John 16:8). Repentance, turning, and faith are three aspects or evidence of salvation in the life of a believer in Christ.

The concept of repentance is a change of one's perspective and point of view, which leads to action demonstrating such change. John the Baptist preached repentance for the forgiveness of sins and required the Jews to show fruits worthy of repentance (Luke 3:3, 8). Jesus's response to the Pharisees who accused Him of communing with publicans and sinners is instructive for it captures the essence of His mission: "They that are whole need not a physician, but they that are sick. I came not to call the righteous, but sinners unto repentance" (Luke 5:31–32). The disease of sin has corrupted the entire human race; no man can heal or cure anyone from this disease, except the Son of God. Christ entered the world, the arena of sin, and effectively fought and defeated sin and Satan, offering this life of deliverance to those who are willing to surrender their life to Him. Jesus forgives, takes away man's sins, and imputes unto them His righteous nature via the gift and power of the Holy Spirit.

Luke associates two other terms with repentance and turning—faith and belief, or trust in God. The use of these terms implies a reliance on someone to provide something men cannot provide for themselves. An instance of this use is the centurion who told Jesus there was no need for Him to visit his home to heal his servant; all he needed to do was speak the word and his servant would be healed. Jesus confessed that such faith exceeded the faith of the Jews (Luke 7:8). On the other hand, a lack of faith or belief on the part of the disciples led them to doubt the ability of God to meet their need; they became fearful (Luke 8:25). The show of repentance was exhibited by the king and people of Nineveh at the message of Jonah. Their actions testified to the fact that they embraced a new perspective of life, revealing their faith in God, hoping and seeking His grace and mercy. God saw their acts of repentance and withheld His hand of judgment (Luke 11:32). Other instances of repentance and turning in Luke are the portrait of the prodigal son, who came to himself and returned to his father a humble and repentant person (Luke 15:11–32), and Zacchaeus the tax collector, who repented of his sins, making a commitment to repay the persons he robbed, (Luke 18:9–14). Luke shows that faith is not passive but active. It believes the promises of God, embraces them as truth, and decisively acts to receive the benefits.

I now wish to briefly list the many benefits of salvation the believer in Christ receives in response to God's invitation. They include the forgiveness of sins, which embraces deliverance from the penalty, guilt, and conscience of sin; the gift of the Holy Spirit, who equips us with power over sin and Satan, granting us deliverance from the power of sin; justification by faith; eternal life in Christ Jesus via the fellowship and guidance of the Holy Spirit; peace with God and the peace of God; the grace and favor of God; and the promise of a reign with Christ when He comes to receive His bride, the church.

CHAPTER 7

GOD'S DISPENSATIONAL DEALINGS WITH MAN PART 3

The Dispensation of Judgment

Most theologians subscribe to a seven-dispensation system. Others see the seven-year period of tribulation that begins after the church is raptured as a dispensation of judgment. I believe the scriptures affirm that the church will be raptured immediately prior to the seven-year tribulation, and I will establish this position in chapter 13. Each dispensation commences with the declaration of specific commands or laws by God for man's compliance. After the rapture of the church, God will open the spiritual eyes of a remnant of the nation of Israel of 144,000—12,000 servants from each tribe. An angel from the east will seal them in their foreheads to protect and empower them for ministry (Rom. 11:25–27; Rev. 7:2–8). Like the church before them, they will then begin to evangelize the nations of the world. I endorse the views of Ron Rhodes, who stated,

> The backdrop to a proper understanding of the 144,000 witnesses during the tribulation is that God had originally chosen the Jews to be His witnesses. He appointed them to share the good news of God with all other people around

the world (Isaiah 42:6; 43:10). The Jews were to be God's representatives to the Gentile peoples. Biblical history reveals that the Jews failed at this task, especially when they didn't recognize Jesus as the divine Messiah. During the future tribulation these 144,000 Jews who become believers in Jesus the Divine Messiah sometime following the rapture, will finally fulfill this mandate from God and be His witnesses all around the world. Their work will yield a mighty harvest of souls (Rev. 7:9–14). Most scholars today agree that Dan's tribe was omitted from the list of tribes, because that tribe was guilty of idolatry on many occasions and as a result, was largely obliterated (Lev. 24:11; Judges 18:1, 30). To engage in unrepentant idolatry is to be cut off from God's blessing. The tribe of Ephraim was also involved in idolatry and paganized worship (Judges 17; Hosea 4:17). This is probably why both tribes were omitted from the list of tribes in Revelation 7. With no further need for the services of the tribe of Levi as priests, God had no further reason for keeping this tribe distinct and separate from the others. This is probably why they were properly included in the tribal listing.[20]

This dispensation will, therefore, commence with the Jewish evangelism. Accordingly, I will regard the period of tribulation as the dispensation of judgment, which serves as the preamble to the Second Coming of Christ and the establishment of His millennial kingdom (Rev. 19:11–16).

The crisis facing nations worldwide would usher in an era of world government that will give rise to the Antichrist, (Rev. 17:17). This will be necessary as no nation will be able to effectively deal with the crises confronting them alone. On earth, men will seek after God to satisfy their need for worship. The abiding Holy Spirit will not be available

---

20 Ron Rhodes, *The End Times in Chronological Order,* 113–114.

to believers as in the church age, when His presence with the body of Christ restrained the power of evil in the world (Rev. 14:6–7). Believers in Christ will suffer great persecution and will be required to adhere to faith in Christ even in the face of death. Only the Christian martyrs will be saved; those who chose to rescind their faith and receive the mark of the beast will experience eternal damnation in hell with the devil and his fallen angels.

The Arab nations will launch a series of attacks against the nation of Israel shortly after the rapture of the church. The Antichrist, who will appear to be a genius providing solutions for some of the world's chaos, will intervene in the wars between Israel and the Arab states and succeed in establishing a peace treaty that will last about three and a half years. The first three and a half years of the tribulation will be a time of relative peace. Toward the end of this era of peace, the Lord will affirm the ministry of the Jews through

> another angel flying in the midst of heaven, having the everlasting gospel to preach unto them that dwell on the earth, and to every nation, and kindred, and tongue and people. Saying with a loud voice, fear God and give glory to Him for the hour of His judgment is come, and worship Him that made heaven and earth and the sea and the fountains of waters. (Rev. 14:6–7)

The dispensation will involve a series of judgments of mankind described in detail in the book of Revelation for their denial of His invitation of salvation, through His Son Jesus the Christ. Three of the four judgments mentioned in the Bible takes place during this period; they are the judgment seat of Christ, or the bema judgment; Jacob's trouble, better known as the tribulation; and the judgment of the nations. The bema judgment of the raptured saints' works will take place in heaven prior to the marriage feast of the Lamb.

The Antichrist, also called the Beast, would sell his soul to the devil, who will fully possess him midway through the tribulation period to unleash his wrath upon the world. He will break the peace treaty and attack and destroy the city of Jerusalem, ravishing the houses and desecrating the newly built temple, causing a third of the population to flee to the mountains (Rev. 12:6; Matt. 24:15–31). God would empower him to make war with the saints, backed by the armies of his collation of nations, and defeat them. He will be given power over all kindreds, tongues, and nations of the world. He will receive a fatal wound during the battle for Jerusalem but will be restored to life by the false prophet, who will also be given power to perform great miracles in his presence. This would lead the Antichrist to make blasphemous statements claiming to be God. The false prophet will erect an image of the Antichrist in the temple court and give life to it so that it speaks in the sight of all (Rev. 13:4–15).

He will institute the mark of the beast as a requirement for all forms of business on earth (Rev. 13:15–17). His partner, the false prophet, will institute world religion, preaching that the Antichrist is God and should be worshipped at the peril of death (2 Thess. 10–12). The sovereign God will, at that time (the beginning of the Great tribulation period), send two witnesses to the streets of Jerusalem to declare His counsel and oppose the activity of the Antichrist and the false prophet. Theologians believe these witnesses will be Enoch and the prophet Elijah, both of whom were translated to heaven, escaping death.

> And I will give power unto my two witnesses, and they shall prophesy a thousand two hundred and three score days, clothed in sackcloth.
>
> These are the two olive trees and the two candlesticks standing before the God of the earth. And if any man hurt them, fire proceed out of their mouth, and devour their enemies, and if any man will hurt them, he must in this manner be killed. These have power to shut heaven, that it rain not, in the days of their prophecy, and have power over waters to turn them to blood, and to smite the earth with all plagues, as often as they will. (Rev. 11:3–6)

The tribulation period, also referred to as Jacob's Trouble, is detailed in the book of Revelation from chapter 6 to chapter 19 and comprises God's judgments via four sets of symbols, the seven seals, seven trumpets, seven signs, and seven vials or bowls. Each set of judgment is preceded by a scene that occurs in the heavens presenting the gospel to the people of the earth and warning of eternal judgment. Each judgment will be progressively worse and will finally culminate in the battle of Armageddon.

I will now provide a summary of these judgments.

The first seal refers to activity of the world's greatest dictator, the Antichrist, to whom the leaders of the world would give power (Rev. 6:1–2; 17:17). The second seal refers to the destruction of worldwide war between nations (Rev. 6:3–4). The third seal refers to the destruction that will inflict the earth via famine (Rev. 6:5–6). The fourth seal refers to the destruction death and hell will inflict on the earth, consuming one-quarter of the world's population (Rev. 6:7–8). The fifth seal refers to the persecution of those who accepted the gospel and refused the mark of the beast and were killed for their faith in the Word of God (Rev. 6:9–10). The sixth seal refers to ecological disaster that shall ravage the earth (Rev. 6:11–14). The seventh seal introduces the trumpet judgments.

The first trumpet refers to the world's greatest hail and fire plague that will destroy one-third of the earth's trees and grass (Rev. 8:7). The second trumpet refers to the greatest oceanic disaster that will turn one-third of the ocean waters to blood, killing one-third of the creatures in the seas and destroying one-third of the ships in the seas (Rev. 8:8–9). The third trumpet refers to the great water pollution that will occur, affecting one-third of the rivers and fountains, making them wormwood bitter, killing many people (Rev. 8:10–11). The fourth trumpet refers to the plague of darkness that will smite the earth when one-third of the sun, moon, and stars become dark (Rev. 8:12). The fifth trumpet refers to the invasion and plague of locusts from the bottomless pit to afflict those who did not have the seal of God on their foreheads for five months (Rev. 9:1–10). The sixth trumpet refers to destruction by four demons, who would possess an army of two hundred thousand, thousands killing one-third of the earth's population (Rev. 9:14–16). The seventh trumpet introduces the seven signs.

The first sign refers to the woman clothed with the sun and the moon under her feet and upon her head a crown of twelve stars, and she, being with child, cried travailing in birth and pained to be delivered (Rev. 12:1–2). The second sign refers to the great red dragon, having seven heads and ten horns and seven crowns upon his heads (Rev. 12:3). The third sign refers to the male child destined to rule all nations with a rod of iron, and he was caught up to God and His throne in heaven (Rev. 12:5–6). The fourth sign refers to the war in heaven, where Archangel Michael and his army will defeat the dragon and his demonic angels and cast them out of the heaven (celestial heaven) (Rev. 12:7–17). The fifth sign refers to the Antichrist (Rev. 13:1–10). The sixth sign refers to the false prophet (Rev. 13:11–18). The seventh sign introduces the vial or bowl judgments (Rev. 15:5–8).

The first vial refers to the world's greatest epidemic (Rev. 16:2). The second vial refers to the contamination of all seas (Rev. 16:3). The third vial refers to the contamination of rivers and fountains by blood in recompense for the slaying of the saints and prophets (Rev. 16:4–7). The fourth vial refers to the scorching of mankind by the heat of the sun (Rev. 16:8–9). The fifth vial refers to the plague of painful putrefying sores (Rev. 16:10–11). The sixth vial refers to the invasion of demons that possess the devil, the Antichrist, and the false prophet to influence the nations to gather in battle against the nation of Israel (Rev. 16:12–14). The seventh vial refers to the Day of God's Wrath, which culminates with the battle of Armageddon (Zach. 14; Jer. 30:7; Rev. 16:15–21; 19:17–21).[21]

The devil, using the body of the Antichrist, will pursue the Jews who escaped into the deserts and mountains to destroy them. The unholy trinity, Satan, the Antichrist/Beast, and the false prophet, will be fully manifested in the final three and a half years of the tribulation, referred to as the Great Tribulation period. The following prophecy of Isaiah will be fulfilled.

> Babylon the glory of kingdoms, the beauty of the Chaldees' excellency shall be as when God overthrew Sodom and Gomorrah. It shall never be inhabited, neither shall it be dwelt in from

---

21   John Callahan, neverthirsty.org/bible-archives.

> generation to generation; neither shall the Arabian pitch tent there; neither shall the shepherds make their fold there. But wild beasts of the desert shall lie there; and their houses shall be full of doleful creatures; and owls shall dwell there, and satyrs shall dance there. (Isa. 13:19–21)

The city of Babylon, the mother of harlots and abominations of the earth and the throne of the Antichrist, will be destroyed by a rebellious group of nations after the seventh angel pours out his vial.

> And there were voices and thunders and lightnings; and there was a great earthquake, such as was not since men were upon the earth, so mighty an earthquake and so great. And the great city was divided into three parts and the cities of the nations fell: and great Babylon came in remembrance before God, to give unto her the cup of the wine of the fierceness of His wrath. (Rev. 16:18–19)

> And a mighty angel took up a stone like a great millstone and cast it into the sea, saying thus with violence shall that great city Babylon be thrown down, and shall be found no more at all. And the light of a candle shall shine no more at all in thee; and the voice of the bridegroom and of the bride shall be heard no more at all in thee; for thy merchants were the great men of the earth; for by thy sorceries were all nations deceived. And in her was found the blood of prophets and of saints and of all that were slain upon the earth. (Rev. 18:21, 23–24)

As the Great Tribulation ends, the battle of Gog and Magog, described in Ezekiel chapters 38–39, will take place in the valley of Jezreel among the mountains of Israel. An examination of the battles described in Daniel 11:40–45, Zechariah 14:2–4, and Revelation 19:15–19 indicates that the Battle of Gog and Magog will be a part of the great battle of Armageddon, which encompasses three phases of military conflicts. Phase 1 is the battle with Gog and Magog, referenced in Ezekiel chapters 38–39. Phase 2 is the battle referenced in Zachariah chapters 12 and 14, and phase 3 is the battle referenced in Revelation 19:11–21, where the Lord will intervene as the armies of the world gather against Israel to destroy the city and nation.[22]

The sovereign God will gather the armies of the nations of the world to fight against the Jews and destroy the city of Jerusalem. He will permit them to capture and plunder half of the city (Zach. 14:1–4) before He intervenes. The Lord Jesus, Lion of the Tribe of Judah, will appear in the clouds with the angelic hosts and the body of Christ and, in His wrath, shall slay the armies gathered against Israel with the sword of His mouth, avenging Himself for the blood of His prophets, the saints, and His people, the Jews in every generation (Ps. 83; Rev. 5:9–11; Zach. 14:12–15).

> And I saw the beast and the kings of the earth, and their armies gathered, to make war against him that sat on the horse and his army. And the beast was taken and with him the false prophet that wrought miracles before him, with which he deceived them that had received the mark of the beast, and them that worshipped his image. These both were cast alive into a lake of fire burning with brimstone. And the remnant was slain with the sword of Him that sat upon the horse, which sword proceeded out from His mouth: and all the fowls were filled with their flesh. (Rev. 19:19–21)

> And I saw an angel come down from heaven, having the key of the bottomless pit and a great chain in his hand. And he laid hold on the dragon, that old serpent, which is the Devil and Satan, and bound him a thousand years, and cast him into the bottomless pit and shut him up, and set a seal upon him, that he should deceive the nations no more, until the thousand years should

---

22   Ibid.

be fulfilled: and after that he must be loosed a little season. (Rev. 20:1–3)

The defeat of the Antichrist and the armies gathered against Israel will be so devastating that the people of Israel will be burying the dead bodies for seven months (Ezek. 39:12). And "they shall set on fire and burn the weapons, both the shields and the bucklers, the bows and the arrows and the hand-staves and the spears, and they shall burn them with fire for seven years" (Ezek. 39:9b).

The Millennial Kingdom

An examination of the prophetic timetable in the book of Daniel indicates that there is an interval of approximately 75 days between the end of the tribulation period and the commencement of the millennial kingdom. The second half of the tribulation lasts only 1,260 days (1,335 1,260 = 75) (Dan. 12:11–12). The removal of the image of the Antichrist that desecrated the temple will likely be completed within 30 day, leaving an interval of 45 days until the commencement of the millennial kingdom.[23]

Noteworthy is the fact that phase 1 of the battle of Armageddon, the conflict with Gog and Magog, where burial of the dead ensued for seven months, would not conflict with the 1,260-day time set for the second half of the tribulation, nor would the Jews' use of various wooden weapons for firewood conflict with the above-mentioned timetable. The members of the unholy trinity would be disposed of in the late stages of the battle of Armageddon, the Antichrist and the false prophet being cast into the lake of fire to be tormented forever while the devil would be bound and cast into and sealed in the bottomless pit for a thousand years. The prophetic calendar indicates that there are three important events that must take place prior to the commencement of the millennial kingdom, namely, the judgment of the nations, the judgment of the twelve tribes of Israel, and the marriage supper of the Lamb (Matt. 25:31–46: Ezek. 20:34–38: Mark 2:19–20).

First, Jesus Himself describes the details of the judgment of the nations in Matthew 25:31–46. Although the judgment is referred to

23   Rhodes, *The End Times in Chronological Order,* 177–78.

as that of nations, it will be done individually and really is a judgment of the Gentile nations of the world. Some scholars misinterpret this judgment to be a part of the great white throne judgment, but a comparison of this text with the white throne judgment text in the book of Revelation reveals many differences, making that impossible. For example, the judgment of nations takes place at the Second Coming of Christ while the white throne judgment takes place after the millennial reign. Second, the judgment of nations is based on the persons' treatment of Jesus's brothers during the tribulation period, while the persons in the white throne judgment will be judged based on their works in their lifetime in the world.

The criteria of judgment for the nations have a lot to do with the fact that the believers in Christ, including the 144,000 Jewish witnesses sealed to evangelize the nations of the world, would find it very difficult to survive rejecting the mark of the beast. They would not be permitted to trade personally and would have to depend on assistance from other people. The persons who rendered assistance to Christ's brothers will be placed into the category of sheep and be rewarded by admission into the Christ's millennial kingdom, while those persons who refused to render assistance to the brothers of Jesus will be condemned to eternal damnation and cast into the lake of fire, prepared for the devil and his demons. Noteworthy is the fact that among the sheep will be Jewish and Gentile believers who came to faith in Christ during the tribulation and refused to accept the mark of the beast.

Addressing the second event, the Judgment of the Twelve tribes of Israel, the prophet Ezekiel (Ezek. 20:34–38) outlines the criteria and methodology on which this judgment will be executed by Christ.[24]

1. It will take place in Jerusalem after the Lord has gathered the tribes from all the nations of the world.

2. Christ will purge, that is, condemn the rebels who refuse to accept His offer of salvation.

3. The believers will be rewarded by admission into the millennial kingdom to enjoy the manifold blessings of the New Covenant.

---

24   Ibid., 184.

4.   The saved believers will possess their natural/mortal bodies and will be able to reproduce children. Although longevity will characterize the millennium reign, mortal Jews and their Gentile counterparts will continue to age and die.

The Lord Himself addresses the third event, the Marriage Supper of the Lamb, repeatedly in the gospels.

In each instance, He referred to Himself as the Bridegroom and the church as the bride. "Can the children of the bridechamber mourn, if the bridegroom is with them? But the days will come when the bridegroom shall be taken from them, and then shall they fast" (Matt. 9:15).

The imagery in scripture of the saints' marriage to Christ is rooted in the Hebrew marriage structure, which comprises three phases.[25] First, the marriage is legally established by the parents of the bride and groom, after which the groom goes to prepare a place to live with his bride in his father's home. Second, the bridegroom comes to claim his bride and takes her to his abode, where the marriage ceremony is conducted. Only members of the immediate families and two witnesses are invited to participate in the ceremony. After the ceremony, a marriage feast is provided to celebrate the new union of the two families. Then finally, there is a marriage supper, to which many relatives, friends, and special guests are invited, which may last several days. The relationship between Christ and the church exhibits these features; two of the three phases are yet to take place.

God anointed Adam with wisdom and power to rule the earth as His representative, but he failed his calling by choosing to violate the commandments of God. God, in His judgment of the serpent and Satan, immediately announced His plan to restore His kingdom and rule in the earth by the Seed of the Woman (Gen. 3:15). Archangel Gabriel announced to the Virgin Mary,

> Behold, thou shall conceive in thy womb and bring forth a son and shall call his name Jesus. Shall be great and shall be called the Son of the Highest; and the Lord God shall give unto Him

---

25   Ibid., 47.

the throne of his father David. And he shall reign over the house of Jacob forever and of his kingdom there shall be no end. (Luke 1:31–33)

Jesus came as the second federal head and the second Adam to purchase the redemption of His Father's creation, animate and inanimate (John 1:11–12; 1 Cor. 15:45–57).

I will examine six events on the prophetic timetable that should precede Christ's establishment of His millennial kingdom in Jerusalem.[26] In chronological order, these are the coming in of the fullness of the Gentiles, the marriage feast of the Lamb, the preaching of the gospel to the whole world, the salvation of all Israel, the Second Coming of the Lord, and the fulfillment of the times of the Gentiles. The coming in of the fullness of the Gentile iniquity will trigger the rapture of the body of Christ (Gen. 15:16; Rom. 11:25), when the dead in Christ shall rise in the first resurrection, then those saints who are alive will be transformed at the appearance of the Lord in the skies and be caught up into heaven (1 Thess. 4:16–17; 1 Cor. 15:51–54). Second, the marriage feast of the Lamb will take place in heaven after the bema seat judgment. These events will be addressed in detail in chapter 14.

Third, the preaching of the gospel to the whole world by the 144,000 Jews who will be sealed by an angel to accomplish this mission in the first three and a half years of the tribulation period (Matt. 24:14; Rev. 7:2–8). Toward the end of that period and shortly before the emergence of the Great Tribulation, the Lord will affirm the ministry of the Jewish missionaries by an angel in the midst of heaven preaching with a loud voice the everlasting gospel to every nation, kindred, tongue, and people, saying, "Fear God and give Glory to Him for the hour of His judgment is come and worship Him that made heaven and earth and the sea and the fountains of waters" (Rev. 14:7).

Fourth, the salvation of all the tribes of Israel will occur in the midst of the battles of Armageddon; the nation will repent at the sight of the Lion of the Tribe of Judah's appearance in the skies with the angelic hosts and the saints of God (Matt. 23:37–39: Hosea 5:15; Rom. 11:14, 25–27). Next will be the Second Advent of Christ Jesus,

---

26   Norman Manson, Biblestudyproject.org/the-millennial.

commonly referred to as His Second Coming to the earth; it will take place at the battle of Armageddon.

Sixth, and last, will be the fulfillment of the times of the Gentile rule of Jerusalem, which began in 586 BC. God gave King Nebuchadnezzar a prophetic dream, which is central to history and Bible prophecy. Daniel, one of his Hebrew advisors, interpreted the dream communicating the succession of world empires that were to oppress Israel and rule the nations of the world. The empires named are Babylon, Media-Persia, Greece, Rome, the Eastern and Western Roman empire, and a collation of ten kingdoms, which will be defeated and destroyed by the Lord Jesus in the battle of Armageddon (Dan. 2:1–45). The reign of all the empires, except for the ten-kingdom collation, has already been fulfilled; the collation will be manifested in the tribulation period and be defeated by the Lord, when He comes to battle for His people, the nation of Israel. "And in the days of these kings shall the God of heaven set up a kingdom, which shall never be destroyed: and the kingdom shall not be left to other people, but it shall break in pieces and consume all these kingdoms and it shall stand forever" (Dan. 2:44).

The Second Coming of Jesus Christ will occur in two different phases. First, He will return in the skies to rapture His church, the body of Christ. The nature of His coming in the air and its purpose will be fully addressed in chapter 13. His second coming to the earth will be a public appearance, for this coming will accomplish a sixfold purpose: to reveal Himself and His Own; to judge the Beast, the false prophet, and their armies; to bind Satan; to save Israel; to judge the nations of the world; to deliver and bless His creation; and to establish His millennial kingdom.[27]

In the first advent, Christ was revealed to men, especially His disciples, with whom He had a special relationship, but He has been hidden from the sight of men for almost two thousand years. He now serves as the Mediator for the race of man and High Priest for His saints in the presence of His Father in heaven (John 1:14; 1 John 1:1–4; 1 Tim. 2:5; Heb. 2:17). The scriptures testify that Jesus will come again to the earth with a host of angels and the redeemed saints from every

---

27   Thiessen, *Lectures in Systematic Theology,* 355–359.

generation, including the patriarchs of the Old Testament, and every eye shall see him (Joel 3:11–12; Zach. 14:5; 1 Thess. 3:13; Rev. 1:7). The angels announced to the disciples, who observed Christ ascending into heaven, "Ye men of Galilee, why stand ye gazing up into heaven, this same Jesus, which is taken up from you into heaven, shall so come in like manner as ye have seen Him go into heaven" (Acts 1:11).

Christ's encounter and defeat of the Beast, the false prophet, and their armies was addressed in the previous section, the dispensation of judgment. The Beast and the false prophet will be cast into the lake of fire shortly before the devil is bound and cast into the bottomless pit for a thousand years (Rev. 19:20; 20; 1–2). When the dragon, the Beast, and their armies seek to surround and destroy the nation of Israel, the Jews will experience the military deliverance they desired for centuries. Having strategically gathered their enemies together, Christ will appear in the clouds with the angelic hosts and saints and unleash His wrath upon the armies with fire from the sword of His mouth (Jer. 30:7; Rev. 19:19–21). Christ's Second Coming and the establishment of His millennial kingdom will fulfill the eschatological covenant promises made to Abraham, Isaac, and Jacob, who will be present with all the saints of God throughout every generation (1 Thess. 4:14–17; 1 John 3:2; 1 Cor. 15:50–54). Christ will not only save Israel but will unite the houses of Israel and Judah and establish a new covenant with them (Isa. 11:11–14; Jer. 33:14–22; 31:31–34; Ezek. 37:18–25).

Following the battle of Armageddon, the Lord will judge the Gentile nations for their treatment of His people during the tribulation period; the people from the nations will be divided into two categories, sheep and goat nations. Because this judgment is for eternal salvation or eternal damnation, it will be made on an individual, not a national, basis. The sheep nations will be praised and rewarded by their admission into the millennial kingdom while the goat nations will be condemned and cast into the lake of fire for their rejection and persecution of the Jews and Gentile believers (Joel 3:17; Matt. 25:31–46; Acts 17:31).

The earth was cursed and made to bring forth thorns and thistles because of man's sin. The creation was corrupted and deviated from its original harmonious and glorious nature (Gen. 3:17– 19). Apostle Paul recorded that "the whole creation groans and travails until now," (Rom.

8:22), but when Christ returns, He will remove the curse and restore His creation to its perfect nature and glory (Isa. 11:1–9; 35:1–2; Ezek. 34:25–31). By statute, all nations will be required to travel to Jerusalem to seek the knowledge of God, worship, pay tribute and celebrate the Feast of Tabernacles; the nations that refuse to attend will receive no rain (Zach. 14:16– 17; Isa. 56:6–7). The image and likeness of God in man will be restored, permitting the animals to dwell harmoniously with mankind and each other again.

> The wolf also shall dwell with the lamb, and the leopard shall lie down with the kid; and the calf and the young lion and the fatling together, and a little child shall lead them. And the cow and the bear shall feed; their young ones shall lie down together; and the lion shall eat straw like the ox. And the suckling child play on the hole of the asp, and the weaned child shall pit his hand on the cockatrice den. They shall not hurt nor destroy in all my holy mountain: for the earth shall be full of the knowledge of the Lord, as the waters. (Isa. 11:6–9)

> Of the increase of His government and peace there shall be no end, upon the throne of David, and upon His kingdom to order it, and to establish it with judgment and with justice from henceforth even forever. (Isa. 9:7)

The foregoing text (Isa. 9:7) will be fulfilled as Christ will rule the entire world with a rod of iron from His throne in the city of Jerusalem. He would have removed every evil influence at this time; the Beast and the false prophet were cast into the lake of fire and the devil was bound for a thousand years.

Except for those believers who survived the tribulation period, the human population of the earth will possess immortal bodies. The tribulation saints will possess their natural bodies. Hence, any occurrence of sin would emanate from the hearts of those believers who possessed natural bodies, being those persons who survived the Great Tribulation and their offspring. Sickness and death will only affect these persons; all sin will be judged instantly by death and banishment to hell, the lake of fire prepared for the devil and his demons (Isa. 65:20; Dan. 9; 24; Rev. 2:27; 21:7–8). The scriptures indicate that there will be a very short time between the millennial reign of Christ and the eternal state; the permissive will of God will culminate in the millennium. Apostle Paul provides readers a clear picture of the final events of this dispensation.

> Then cometh the end, when He shall have delivered up the kingdom to God, even the Father, when He shall have put down all rule all authority and power. For He must reign, till He hath put down all enemies under His feet. The last enemy that shall be destroyed is death… And when all things shall be subdued unto Him, then shall the Son also Himself be subject unto Him that put all things under Him, that God may be all in all. (1 Cor. 15:24–26, 28)

At the close of the millennium, the devil will be released from the bottomless pit for a brief period to try the nations of the earth for the last time. He will influence the armies of Gog and Magog to gather to attack Jerusalem, but they shall be consumed by fire from heaven.

> And shall go out to deceive the nations which are in the four quarters of the earth…to gather them together to battle the number of whom is as the sand of the sea. And they went up on the breath of the earth, and compassed the camp of the saints about, and the beloved city: and fire came down from God out of heaven, and devoured them. (Rev. 20:8–9)

The devil will be judged together with all his demons and cast into the lake of fire and brimstone to join the Beast and the false prophet, where they will be tormented forever (2 Peter 2:4: Rev. 20:7–10). After God has cast the unholy trinity and all their demons into the lake of fire, the second resurrection will occur. Jesus said, "Marvel not at this: for the hour is coming, in the which all that are in the graves shall hear His voice sand shall come forth; they that have done good, unto the resurrection of life; and they that have done evil, unto the resurrection of damnation" (John 5:28–29).

Apostle John provided the details on the criteria and methodology of the great white throne judgment.

> I saw a great white throne and Him that sat on it, from whom face the earth and the heaven fled away…And I saw the dead, small and great, stand before God and the books were open, and another book was opened, which is the book of life: and the dead were judged out of those things which were written in the books, according to their works. And the sea gave up the dead which were in it; and death and hell delivered the dead which were in them; and they were judged every man according to their works. And death and hell were cast into the lake of fire. And whosoever was not found written in the Book of life was cast into the lake of fire. (Rev. 20:11–15)

The Eternal State

Dispensations cover a specific period, but the eternal state will exist eternally and cannot be accurately termed a dispensation. Nevertheless, I choose to locate it within this chapter because it exhibits the success of God's permissive dealings with mankind, the fulfillment of every facet of His redemptive plan and programs (Eph. 4:12–13; 1 John 3:2). At this time, the second resurrection will occur, the resurrection of the unsaved dead, those persons who died in their sins. Christ will appear in the clouds seated on a great white throne to judge the world according to the records of heaven of their deeds in life. The sea, death, and hell will surrender their dead, and everyone will be judged for their deeds; those persons whose names are not found in the Lamb's Book of Life will be cast into the lake of fire and will be tormented forever.

King David recorded, "The Lord said unto my Lord, sit thou at my right hand, until I make thine enemies thy footstool" (Ps. 110:1).

Death and hell will also be cast into the lake of fire for all eternity (Rev. 20:11–15). Having defeated all His enemies, mortal and immortal, the enemies of Israel, sin, Satan, death, and hell and every knee having bowed and tongue confessed Him as Lord and God, Christ Jesus will deliver the kingdom of the world into the hands of God the Father so that the Father Himself can be all in all (Phil. 2:10–11). That act of Christ will usher in the eternal state, which will comprise a new heaven, a new earth, and a new Jerusalem (Isa. 65:17).

In chapter 2, I established the fact that there are three heavens. The new heavens referred to in the eternal state will not include Paradise, the dwelling place of God, but the celestial and atmospheric heavens (Isa. 66:22). I endorse the views of Clarence Thiessen expressed hereunder.

> The heaven and earth are called new but that does not mean new in the absolute sense, for the earth abides forever, Ps. 104:5; Eccl. 1:4. The passages that speak of the earth passing away, Matt. 5:18; Heb. 1:10–13; Rev. 21:1 do not signify a passing into non-existence but rather a transition. Neither heaven or earth will be annihilated; as in the millennium, they will be regenerated and sanctified, Matt. 19:28; 2 Peter 3:10–13.[28]

God's perfection is infinite. There is no room for improvement; hence, the new heaven could not imply Paradise, the abode of God. Jesus's reference of heaven and earth passing away had no inference to Paradise. Satan is referred to as prince of the powers of the air because he has set up his kingdom in the celestial and atmospheric heavens, but he will be cast down to the earth during the tribulation period by Michael and his host of angels (Eph. 2:2; Rev. 12:7–9). Christ will fulfill the prophecy recorded by Daniel.

> To finish the transgression, to make an end of sins, and to make reconciliation for iniquity and to bring in everlasting righteousness and to seal up the vision and prophecy and to anoint the Most Holy. (Dan. 9:24)

---

28 Thiessen, *Lectures in Systematic Theology*, 402.

Hence, there will be no sin, no evil, no sickness, no pain, no death, no sadness, no strife, but love, fullness of joy, worship, praise, thanksgiving, glory, and honor to God in the eternal state. For the knowledge of the Lord shall fill the earth even as it did in the millennial kingdom. There will be no night and no need for the sun or the moon, for the glory of God and the Lamb shall be the light therein (Rev. 21:23–25). The animals and people will dwell together in harmony as in the millennial kingdom, and there shall no hurt come to anyone. The earth's population in the eternal state will be immortal beings. Apostle John exhorts believers that they are now the sons of God and does not yet appear what they shall be, but know that when Christ appears, they shall be like Him for they shall see Him as He is (1 John 3:2).

Having examined the general features and atmosphere in the new heaven and new earth, I will now examine the new Jerusalem. The apostle John indicates that he saw a new heaven and new earth and there was no sea; I understand that John wanted to record the majestic transformation that took place in the heavens and earth before addressing the emergence of the New Jerusalem, which he saw fashioned by God in heaven and presented to mankind, somewhat like the Garden of Eden was presented to Adam and Eve (Rev. 21:1–2; Gen. 2:8–15). I observe five parallels between the Garden of Eden and the New Jerusalem, namely, the perfection of God's handiwork is evident everywhere, the glory of God is resident there, the Tree of Life is there, a river of life is there, and the Lord God will establish a throne there and fellowship with His people there (Rev. 21; Gen. 1).

Addressing events of the last days, Jesus comforted His disciples with these words,

> Let not your heart be troubled, you believe in God, believe also in me. In my Father's house there are many mansions, if it were not so, I would have told you. I go to prepare a place for you. And if I go and prepare a place for you, I will come again, and receive you unto myself, that where I am you may be also. (John 14:1–3)

Christ is preparing a unique home for His people, where they will dwell together forever. I endorse the view of many theologians who are of the view that Christ will take the raptured church to that place. That place of abode will be adorned with the throne of Christ as He reigns with all His saints from every generation of mankind, including the patriarchs of old and the saints martyred during the tribulation period. I endorse the views of J. Hampton Keathley III, who stated,[29]

> Because of its heavenly nature it may be like a satellite city which will orbit or hover above the earth and will finally settle upon it during the millennium. This idea of Jerusalem as a satellite city during the millennium is of course only by implication and not a definite statement. If this is so, then this heavenly city will be withdrawn at the end of the millennium, in connection with the destruction of the old heaven and earth. Make ready as a bride adorned for her husband, compares the city to a bride, but this does not limit the city to the church. All saints will ultimately live in this city. The figure of the bride simply emphasizes the permanency as marriage is designed to be permanent, so this will be our permanent or eternal abode, as a bride is beautifully adorned for her wedding, so this stresses the beauty of this city as it is adorned for the saints, and as the bride is to be pure, it portrays the purity of the holy city. (Heb. 11:10, 16)

The dwelling place of the Lord and His saints will need no improvement from its state in the millennium; hence, it may be lifted from the old earth and be presented again to the new earth in the eternal state.

---

29   J. Hampton Keathley III, bible.org/eternal state.

CHAPTER 8

THE PAULINE CATEGORIZATION OF MAN

The sovereign God releases knowledge to the race of man consistent with His divine program and purposes. Apostle Paul was given the revelation of God's New Covenant with the race of man, manifested in the dispensation of grace.

> I, Paul, the prisoner of Jesus Christ for you Gentiles, if you have heard of the dispensation of the grace of God, which is given me to you, how that by revelation He made known unto me the mystery, whereby when you read you may understand my knowledge in the mystery of Christ, which in other ages was not made known unto the sons of men, as it is now revealed unto his holy apostles and prophets by the Spirit. That the Gentiles should be fellow-heirs, and of the same body, and partakers of His promise in Christ by the gospel. (Eph. 3:1–6)

Saul, a zealous persecutor of the saints of the early church in Jerusalem, was on his way to capture saints from another city when the Lord Jesus stuck him blind on the road to Damascus and revealed Himself to him, forcefully announcing that he was persecuting the members of His body. The manifestation of God's supernatural power brought Saul into total submission and conversion. God, knowing his heart, chose him for service in His kingdom, forgave him, and empowered him for the work of the ministry, changing his name from Saul to Paul. In commissioning him, the Lord said,

> I have appeared unto you for this purpose, to make thee a minister and a witness both of these things which thou has seen and of those things in the which I will appear unto thee, delivering thee from the people and from the Gentiles unto whom now I send thee. To open their eyes and to turn them from darkness to light and from the power of Satan to God, that they may receive forgiveness of sins and inheritance among them which are sanctified by faith that is in me. (Acts 26:16–18)

The saints of the early church were skeptical about Paul's conversion until the intervention of Barnabas, who befriended him. He got to know him personally and affirmed that he was a true minister of the gospel of Jesus Christ. In examining the operations of Satan in the lives of mankind, Apostle Paul reveals the three primary enemies of the soul: Satan, self, and the world system, working in covert manifestations, namely, the flesh and individuality. Satan, the devil, is the archenemy of God and the people of God. His plan against the race of man, the object of God's love, is to kill, steal, and destroy as many persons as possible (John 10:10).

The Bible makes several references to the flesh. In the Old Testament and some aspects of the New Testament, the word is used as a designation for humankind, blood relatives, or for all living things. God warned that the flood He was about to bring on the earth would destroy "all flesh" (Gen. 6:17). The prophet Joel prophesied that God would outpour His Spirit upon "all flesh" (Joel 2:28–32; Acts 2:17–21). In the New Testament, especially the Pauline epistles, the term *flesh* is used as a designation for the sinful nature of mankind. The term *flesh*, in this text, refers to fallen human nature that is incapable of conforming to the holy requirements of God (Rom. 7:5, 18; 8:3–9; Gal. 3:3).

It refers to the unaided human effort, mere human effort without the power of the Holy Spirit. The flesh presents sin a foothold in the life of believers (Rom. 8:3–4; 9; Gal. 5:16–17). Paul explains that the flesh and the Spirit of God are consistently engaged in a conflict in the life of believers. This necessitates the believers' denial of sinful desires coupled with a pattern of consistent submission to the Holy Spirit for spiritual growth and maturity (Rom. 8:13; Gal. 2:19–21; Col. 3:5). Accordingly, the Pauline idiom of flesh refers to the manifestation of the enthroned "self" in the life of a believer (Luke 9:23–24).

The term *world* and its adjectival form *worldly* in scripture refers to the systems of world civilization that conflict with the teachings of the Word of God. More concisely, it refers to the culture, belief, and value systems of nations, cities, and communities that contradict the counsel of God (1 John 2:15–17; 1 Cor. 6:9–13; Rev. 21:8). The terminology often employed in the Old Testament is conduct "like the heathen nations" (Isa. 55:6–9; Lev. 18:2–5; Ezek. 20:32–38; Jer. 10:2–6).

The Greek philosopher Plato promulgated that the body of man was inherently evil and was an obstacle to spirituality, but the teachings of the Word of God, both in the Old and New Testaments, contradict that view. On the sixth day of God's creative works, He created man in His image and after His likeness, blessed them, gave them power and authority over all the works of his hand in the earth, and pronounced that all was very good in His sight (Gen. 1:26–31). Apostle Paul communicates that believers' bodies are the temples of the Holy Spirit and the instruments of God and the body of Christ on earth. The body of the Spiritfilled believer becomes the arm of God, salt and light in fulfillment of God's divine purposes on earth. In his teaching, Apostle Paul outlined that mankind may be categorized into three groups, depending on their response to the ministry of the Holy Spirit. These groups are the spiritual man, the natural man, and the carnal man. Author will now examine these groups.

The Spiritual Man

In his dialogue with Nicodemus, Jesus stated,

> Verily, verily I say unto thee, except a man be born again he cannot see the kingdom of God...

> Verily, verily I say unto thee, except a man be born of water and of the Spirit, he cannot enter into, the kingdom of God. That which is born of the flesh is flesh and that which is born of the Spirit is spirit. Marvel not that I say unto thee, ye must be born again. (John 3:3, 5–7)

In my examination of the constitution of man (in chapter 4), I addressed the functions of the spirit of man, stating that it provides "God consciousness" in a threefold relationship facilitated by the person of the abiding Holy Spirit. Chapter 3 established that God created man in His image and after His likeness to have the privilege and pleasure of his fellowship and to receive his worship (Isa. 43:7; 1 John 1:3). Mankind is two-thirds spiritual, his spirit and soul being spiritual in nature. The body, the sole physical component of man, gets its life and energy from the spirit.

Of the three components, the soul of man is the real person and not the body or the spirit. Hence, Jesus was referring to the birthing of the soul of man in His dialogue with Nicodemus (John 3:3–7; Ezek. 18:4; Eccl 12:7). The soul of man has its own life and leaves the body from time to time; that's why a person's dreams seem so real. Effective demonstrations of this fact are the narratives of the prophet Elijah raising the dead lad and Jesus raising the dead damsel, appended hereunder.

> And he stretched himself upon the child three times, and cried unto the Lord, and said O Lord my God, I pray thee, let this child's soul come into him again. And the Lord heard the voice of Elijah; and the soul of the child came into him again, and he revived. And Elijah took the child and brought him down out of the chamber into the house and delivered him unto his mother; and Elijah said, see thy son is alive. (1 Kings 17:21–23)

> When Jesus heard it, He answered him saying, Fear not, believe only and she shall be made whole. And when He came into the house, he

suffered no man to go in save Peter, James and John and the father and mother of the maiden. And all wept and bewailed her, but He said Weep not she is not dead but is asleep. And they laughed Him to scorn, knowing that she was dead. And He put them all out, and took her by the hand and called saying, Maid arise. And her spirit came again, and she arose straightway, and He commanded to give her meat. And her parents were astonished but He charged them that they should tell no man what was done. (Luke 8:50–56)

When someone accepts Jesus Christ as their Savior, God the Father sends the gift of the Holy Spirit to reside in that person's spirit to guide and govern their life. The dominating influence of the Holy Spirit causes that person's soul to experience the rebirth Jesus spoke about, being born again with the very nature and life of God, Zoe. No wonder the apostle Paul said, "If anyone among you do not have the Spirit of Christ, they are not a true believer, and need to be saved; and if any man be in Christ, he is a new creature, old things are passed away; behold all things are become new" (Rom. 8:9(b), 2 Cor. 5:17). The new birth provides the believer new power of vision and inner knowledge by which he discerns God's guidance. God's sovereignty was there all the time, but individuals cannot discern it until they receive His nature themselves. The fisherman is comfortable at sea because the nature of the sea is in him; likewise, it is the nature of God in the believer that permits him to experience a lasting relationship with God and the people of God (1 John 1:1–4; Ps. 23).

The soul of man is composed of the will, mind, and emotions, but the decision-maker is always the will. The emotions convey information from the five senses to the mind to influence the decisions, but the Holy Spirit constantly guides and warns the will against choices that are contrary to the Word and Will of God. Accordingly, the mind becomes a battlefield between the kingdom of God and the kingdom of darkness via the fleshly carnal nature that opposes the promptings of the Holy Spirit. However, when the believer choses to submit to the government of the Holy Spirit, he commands his soul to yield to and worship the

Lord God and grows in relationship with the Lord. The spiritual man exhibits a consistent pattern of obedience to the government of the Holy Spirit, which produces spiritual growth manifested in a victorious Christlike life (Rom. 8:14; Ps. 1; 1 John 5:18–20).

God's purpose and design in the creation of man was for his soul and body to be controlled by the spirit, in union with the person of the Holy Spirit. Concisely, Paul states that the spiritual man, by an act of his will, has enthroned Christ on the throne of his heart by the power of the Holy Spirit. For the rule and power of the spirit of life in Christ Jesus sets the believer free from the rule and power of sin and death (Rom. 8:2). His deliverance is manifested in six characteristics: he has a lifestyle and value system that separates him from the pattern of the world; he embraces a belief system that worships and honors the God of Abraham, Isaac and Jacob; he prays often; he expresses love for people in word and deeds by giving of his time and substance from time to time; he forgives those that offend him often; and he regards God as his source and would occasionally lay aside his food to seek the counsel and fellowship of God (1 John 2:15–17; Ps. 1: Jer. 17:7–8; 1 Cor. 13:1–8; Matt. 6:1–24).

The spiritual man's hope is in the Lord; he recognizes that God is the architect of his circumstances and is not easily moved by the events of life. He is anchored by the many promises of God, which govern his life (Matt. 6:33; John 16:33; Rom. 8:28–39).

The Natural Man

The natural man is that person who is not saved. He has not surrendered his life to the Lord but may be a church member. He may have been accepted as a member of a congregational church. Because of Adam's sin, unregenerate man's spirit sunk into servitude to his soul, which, in turn, is controlled by his body. The natural man's soul is ruled by the self,[30] and his passions govern his body. He embraces the culture, belief, and value system of the world and treasures the wisdom and counsel of man above that of God. Oswald Chambers states,[31]

> Individuality is the hard outer layer surrounding
> the inner spiritual life. Individuality shoves

---

30 Watchman Nee, *Secrets to Spiritual Power*, 263.
31 Oswald Chambers, *My Utmost for His Highest, Devotional*, Dec. 11.

others aside, separating, and isolating people. We see it as the primary characteristic of a child, and rightly so. When we confuse individuality with the spiritual life, we remain isolated, this shell of individuality is God' created natural covering designed to protect the spiritual life. But our individuality must be yielded to God so that our spiritual life may be brought forth into fellowship with Him. Individuality counterfeits spirituality, just as lust counterfeits love. God designed human nature for Himself, but individuality corrupts human nature for its own purposes. The characteristics of individuality are independence and self-will. We hinder our spiritual growth more than any other way by continually asserting our individuality.

The natural man's life is governed by his mind. The self is enthroned on the throne of his heart. He naturally seeks after his own welfare and, hopefully, that of his loved ones. Paul states that the natural man cannot receive or know the counsel of God because his mind has been blinded by the devil, the god of the world system. Hence, they seem foolish to him, the eyes of his understanding being dull to spiritual things (1 Cor. 2:14; 2 Cor. 4:4). The natural man's hope and security is in his own hands. He works and seeks to secure himself, using the available systems of the world, namely, insurance, stock market and other financial investments, real estate, among other options. He does not seriously consider his eternal existence and destiny; his focus is his welfare and estate in this life (Luke 9:23–26; 16:19–31; Matt. 6:19–34).

The Carnal Man

The carnal man in Pauline teaching is a born-again believer who has entered a backslidden state, yielding to his fleshly passions. The Word of God is quick and powerful, sharper than a two-edged sword, piercing even to the dividing asunder of the soul and spirit and is a discerner of the thoughts and intents of the heart (Heb. 4:12). The carnal man undervalues the Word of God and does not delight and abide in it. Hence, he lacks the power to overcome temptations (Ps. 1). The believer in Christ is liberated from the power of fleshly passions by identification with the atoning work of Jesus on the cross of Calvary (Gal. 2:20; Rom. 6:7). By that act of faith, the believer overcomes temptations as he submits to the government of the Holy Spirit. Failure of such submission permits the self to be enthroned on the throne of his heart, suppressing the influence of the Holy Spirit in his decision-making. Accordingly, the belief and value system of the carnal man are compromised by habitual fleshly indulgence.

The carnal man may be attending church regularly and may even be involved in some aspects of ministry, but he has not surrendered his life to the discipline of the Word of God (Luke 9:23–25; 1 John 2:15–17). He exhibits a lifestyle that resembles that of the natural man, except for his religious activities. Accordingly, this person needs to repent and turn from his sins like the prodigal son to find favor with God (Luke 15:11–24; Matt. 13:18–23).

The believer's union with Christ in His death signifies that it is an accomplished fact in his spirit. What a believer must do is bring this sure death out of his spirit and apply it to his body each time his lusts are aroused. The flesh is Satan's workshop, his realm of operation. If the flesh, as a whole and not in part, is under the power of the death of the Lord, Satan is unemployed.[32]

Should the carnal man die in his sins, that is, should he continue to live a life governed by his fleshly passions, he will go to a lost eternity in hell (Rom. 6:23; Rev. 21:8).

---

32   Nee, *Secrets to Spiritual Power*, 264.

CHAPTER 9

EXAMINATION OF THE ELEVEN THEORIES OF ORIGIN PART 1

I will examine the eleven theories of origin expounded and will endeavor to state the theory, the person who promulgated it and the date, and where possible, the identity of the leading philosophers who support it. I will also state how the theory compares with the teachings of the Bible. My position will always be the position established by the holy scriptures.

The Theory of Preexistence

This theory states that the soul of man existed in some form before his birth and entered his body at an early stage of development in the womb, perhaps at conception. The identity of the philosopher who promulgated this theory is not known, but it must be one of the very early philosophers as Plato, Philo, and Origen supported it. Plato supported it because it explained the way people may acquire knowledge outside of the five senses. Philo supported it because it agrees with his view of the soul's imprisonment in the body. Origen supported it because it provides an explanation of the disparity of states of being and health (the presence of physical, mental, or learning disabilities or deformities) in which some children are born. Origen viewed these life-altering conditions or states of being as divine judgment for acts of self-determination committed in a previous existence.

The Bible, however, contradicts these views as it states that all sin and causes of death originated from Adam's sinful act. His act corrupted the very nature of mankind, for the whole race was party to Adam's sin, being in his loins (Rom. 5:12 1 Cor. 15:21–22). David, in repentance after one of his public sins, confessed, "In sin did my mother conceive me." Paul states that all have sinned and come short of the glory or requirement of God (Ps. 51:5; Rom. 3:23).

As regards the fact that man often receives knowledge intuitively, the entire Bible, from Genesis to Revelation, illustrates the principle and practice of God to provide mankind, saved and unsaved, knowledge, wisdom, and understanding in order that he may accomplish His divine purposes. Adam in the naming of the animals (Gen. 2:19–20), Moses in delivering Israel from the Egyptian bondage (Exod. 14:15–18), Joshua in conquering Jericho (Josh. 6:2–5), Paul on the road to Damascus (Acts 9:4–6), and Peter on his mission to Cornelius's household (Acts 10:10–22) are all examples.

The Theory of Evolution

Philosophers, theologians, and scientists in every generation have always sought to explain the origin, history, and variety of life-forms on earth. During the Scientific Revolution in Western Europe during the seventeenth and eighteenth centuries, the predominant view of the origin of man and the universe was the biblical account of divine creation, which states that God created every organism on earth, basically as they appear today. From then, however, philosophers and secular scientists mainly have been pursuing the theory of evolution. Philosophers who supported this theory include French orator and priest Nicholas Malebranche (1638–1715) and Greek and Roman philosophers Anaximander, Empedocles, and Lucretius. In the midnineteenth century, a modern theory of evolution was shaped by British naturalist Charles Darwin in his book *On the Origin of the Species by Means of Natural Selection*, published in 1859. Evolution is an atheistic doctrine that tries to explain the presence of life on earth without a Divine Creator.[33]

---

33   Roger G. Gallop, *Evolution the Greatest Deception in Modern* History, xiii.

Evolutionists believe the big bang created the universe from nothing ten to twenty billion years ago. Our solar system formed about five billion years ago. Single-celled organisms formed from nonliving matter three to five billions years ago.Multicellular organisms slowly evolved about one billion years ago. Humans evolved from higher life-forms one hundred and eighty-five thousand to two million years ago, and modern civilization emerged within the last five thousand to ten thousand years. This doctrine holds that man descended from the apes, all vertebrates descended from fish, all fish descended from invertebrates, and all life descended from single-celled organisms, which arose spontaneously from nonliving chemicals.[34]

The theory of evolution states that all living organisms, from the microscopic bacteria to plants, insects, and other animals, share a common ancestor; species that are closely related share a recent common ancestor, while all other species have a common ancestor in the distant past. Evolutionists claim that the chimpanzee is closely related to man and, therefore, has a common ancestor with man dating back some seven million years.

Evolutionists generally put forward six arguments in support of their hypothesis based on comparative anatomy, vestigial or obsolete organs, embryology, biochemistry, paleontology, and genetics. The similarities between man and the higher vertebrata cannot be viewed as conclusive evidence in support of evolution as an equally strong case can be made that they are indicators of a common creator considering that they dwell in the same or similar environment. Likewise, the similarities in the biochemical composition of living organisms can clearly be attributed to the fact that they live on similar life-support systems of acids, proteins, and water.

Medical research has discovered that organs, such as the tonsils and appendix, which were thought to be useless in the body, are, in fact, serving specific latent functions and should not be removed. Other studies also recently revealed that contrary to the earthworm theory postulated by evolutionists, the heart of the embryo develops before the circulatory system. As regards the genetics argument, research has proven that mutations in any species are minute and negligible when compared to the gene pool; moreover, mutations tend to render the

---

34   Ibid., 1.

organism more vulnerable to the environment, thereby reducing its chances of survival.

The Bible clearly teaches that God made man in His own image and after His likeness; male and female made He them. After forming the body of Adam from the dust of the ground, God breathed the breath of life into his nostrils, and man became, at that moment, a living soul (Gen. 1 and 2). Paul states that "all flesh is not the same, there is a flesh of men, another of beast, another of fish and another of birds" (1 Cor. 15:39).

The Traducian Theory

This is the biblical theory or account of the origin of all things and beings, which is detailed in the book of Genesis and referred to throughout the Bible. This account, of course, was affirmed by all the Old Testament prophets, Jesus in His earthly ministry, and all the apostles and writers of the New Testament. The theory states that God created humans immediately in Adam, both soul and body, and both were propagated from him by natural generation. Tertullian, Shedd, Gregory of Nyssa, and Augustine are believed to have supported this theory together with the Lutheran and evangelical theologians.

This theory regards man as a distinctive species, male and female, perpetuating themselves as wholes. The account in Genesis 2:1–3 records that the process of creation was completed on the sixth day, and God said it was very good. This being the case, God surely has not been continuously creating souls as people are conceived momentously throughout the world. This theory affirms the creation of the souls of man on the basis of the testimony of the scriptures and the law of creation, for the origin of our soul ought to be the same as the soul of Adam, not only because we ought to bear his image, but also because his creation, as the first individual of the species, is an example of the formation of all men (1 Cor. 15:47–48). The soul of Adam was created immediately by God, who breathed into his nostrils the breath of life (Gen. 2:7). Thus, it is evident that his soul was not produced from potent material but came to him extrinsically through creation and was infused into the body by the breath of God Himself. For as the soul of Adam was created out of nothing, so also are the souls of his posterity, and as his body was formed of the dust of the earth, so also our bodies from seed, which itself is earthly and material. Therefore, the mode of action with respect to Adam was singular, yet the nature of the thing is the same. This is confirmed by the production of Eve herself, whose origin, as the body, is described as from a rib of Adam, but of the soul, no mention is made. Hence, it is plainly gathered that the origin of her soul was not different from that of the soul of Adam; otherwise, Moses would not be silent on the matter. Adam himself would have mentioned the origin. He would have declared it specially; he would have said not only "this is bone of my bones" but "soul of my soul" (Gen. 2:23). Finally, if Adam's soul and ours had a different origin, they could not be said to be of the same species, because his was from nothing. Ours cannot be from a preexisting material, completely dissimilar.[35]

The Traducian theory best supports the biblical account for other reasons also. It views Adam and Eve not as representatives of mankind, for they were the whole human race. Accordingly, all mankind sinned in Adam and share the guilt, not for Adam's sin, but for their own individual sins committed against the laws of God. Truly, if anyone says they have no sin, the truth is not in them, for all have sinned and come short of God's holy standard. Jesus said, "Be ye holy as God your Father in Heaven is Holy." Adam's sinful nature was propagated to his seed; all mankind was shaped in iniquity, and in sin, all men were conceived (Rom. 3:23; Ps. 51:5; Job 14:4).

---

35   Matthew McMahon, apuritansmind.com/creationism, or Traducianism.

CHAPTER 10

EXAMINATION OF THE ELEVEN THEORIES OF ORIGIN PART 2

The Pelagian Theory

This theory was promulgated by a British monk who rejected the biblical doctrines of original sin and predestination. Pelagius believed and taught that Adam's sin was personal and affected only himself; his theory states that every soul is created by God individually and is not corrupted in any way by sin or guilt. It claims that Adam's sin was not inherited by his descendants, and if it affected them at all, it must be only by way of a bad example.

The implication of this teaching is gross, as it negates the foundational truths of the Bible, including God's pronouncement and judgment of sin together with His plan of salvation to reconcile man unto Himself. Pelagius postulated his doctrines at Rome in AD 409. This theory further states that God created man free from corruption of any sort, giving him the faculty of free will and the ability to understand and obey Him like Adam possessed in the Garden of Eden. Pelagius claimed that the grace of God is present everywhere and mankind know the will of God and can fulfill His commandments by his own efforts. He taught that man can be saved or please God, as he put it, both by grace and by works, that is, by merit without any further impartation by God.

Celestius, a follower of Pelagius, supported this heresy; they were both condemned by two Councils of African Bishops in 416 and again at Carthage in 418 and were finally excommunicated in 418. Julian of Eclanum also defended this but was condemned at the Second Council of Ephesus in 431. A similar doctrine known as the semi-Pelagainism flourished in Southern Gaul until they were condemned at the Second Council of Orange in 529.

The Bible contradicts every aspect of this theory, for it teaches that in Adam, the entire human race sinned; the very nature of man was immediately corrupted. Every child not only inherited a sinful nature but found himself sinning naturally on the advent of moral consciousness. Paul sums it up in when he said, "Knowing that a man is not justified by the works of the law, but by the faith of Jesus Christ, even we have believed in Jesus Christ that we might be justified, for by the works of the law shall no flesh be justified" (Gal. 2:16). Again he states, "For I know that in me dwelleth no good thing. For the good that I would I do not; but the evil which I would not, that I do. Now if I do that I would not, it is no more I that do it, but sin that dwelleth in me" *Rom. 7:18–20). James echoes the words of Jesus when he said, "Whosoever shall keep the whole law, and yet offend in one point, he is guilty of all" (James 2:10).

The Arminian Theory

James Arminian (1603–1609), the promulgator of the Arminian theory, was a Dutch reformed pastor and theologian from the University of Leiden. There are considerable differences in the doctrinal positions among theologians who support this theory. The Greek Orthodox and Methodist denominations support this theory. This theory states that all men received a corrupt nature from Adam; hence, all humans are unable to fulfill God's will without special divine help. This inability, however, is viewed to be physical and intellectual, but not volitional. This theory states that although mankind received a corrupt nature from Adam and experienced guilt, that guilt and culpability was removed by the gift of grace through Jesus Christ.

The Bible, however, contradicts this theory for it clearly states that all have sinned and come short of the glory of God; it affirmed that we all sinned in Adam and are guilty before God even before we commit a personal sin. Scriptures also teach that because God gave man free will, He will not contravene the will of any man by forcefully bestowing on him any special influence of grace. Jesus Himself, teaching, said, "*If* any man will come after me let him deny himself take up his cross and follow me" (Matt. 16:24, emphasis here is on the prepositional conjunction "if "). His dialogue with Nicodemus is applicable here also. "Verily, verily I say unto thee, except a man be born of water and of the Spirit, he cannot enter the kingdom of God. That which is born of flesh is flesh and that which is born of the Spirit is spirit" (John 3:5–6).

The Calvinistic Theory

This theory was promulgated by the theologian John Calvin and primarily focuses more attention on the original sin than any other school of theology. The theory states that there is a firm connection between Adam's sin and the entire human race; his sin was not the isolated act of an individual but was also our personal sin. He believed and taught that every man and woman received a corrupt nature, perhaps from the point of conception, meaning even before birth. Therefore, we all received an inherited tendency toward sin in addition to the fact that we are guilty of Adam's sin, for we participated in it. Hence, death, the penalty of sin, has been passed on to us from Adam.

This theory is supported by the Bible and basically agrees with and is parallel to the Traducian theory addressed earlier, although the Traducian theory doesn't regard Adam's sin as personal to his seed. Supporting scriptures for this theory are identical with those shared with regard to the Traducian theory (Rom. 3:23; Ps. 51:5; Job 14:4). Calvin agreed with Martin Luther on justification by faith and the sole authority of the scriptures. On the sacrament of the Lord's supper, he took a position between the radical Swiss and the Lutheran view. Thus, he believed that the body of Christ was not present everywhere but that His spirit was universal and that there was a genuine communion with the risen Lord. Calvin, likewise, took a middle view on music and art. He favored congregational singing of the Psalms which became a characteristic practice of the Huguenots in France and the Presbyterians in Scotland and the New World.

The Theory of Mediate Imputation

The theory of mediate imputation states that all men are born physically and morally depraved, and this corrupt nature is the source of all sin. The theory also states that man receives the corrupt nature by natural propagation from Adam and because of his sin. It views Adam's sin as imputed mediately and not immediately. John Murray, who promulgated this theory, argues that the obligation to satisfy justice may be imputed only on the grounds of a logical antecedent or demerit.[36]

Because this theory does not recognize us as participating in Adam's sin, it makes depravity the cause of the imputation and contradicts the biblical position. The Bible teaches that we all sinned in Adam, that is, we participated in the act of sin together with Adam. God, who dwells outside of time, saw the entire race of man in Adam's loins at the time of his sin. Secondly, this theory removes the parallelism between Adam and Jesus, who came as the Second Adam or the Second Federal Head of the race of man (1 Cor. 15:45–49 and Rom. 5:12).

---

36   Sam Storms, samstorms.org, mediate or immediate imputation.

CHAPTER 11

EXAMINATION OF THE ELEVEN THEORIES OF ORIGIN PART 3

The Realistic Theory

This theory states that mankind was physically and substantially in the loins of Adam when he sinned and can, therefore, be viewed as participating in the act with him. Corruption and guilt came because of sin, a state of being Adam transmitted to all his descendants. Authors supporting this theory include Thucydides, Niccolò Machiavelli, Thomas Hobbes, Jean-Jacques Rousseau, and Max Webber.

I support this theory because it aligns with the teachings of the scriptures, for Adam sinned before the conception of his first child, so in propagating after his kind, he propagated his corrupt nature. As the scriptures indicate that the seed of man is in his loins, the reverse is also implied, that is, that the father lives on in the person of his seed, though not in a personal or conscious way. This has to do with man's main purpose in life. God Himself inferred in the statement that He is the God of Abraham, Isaac, and Jacob. The mission is to be continued by man's seed. This is God's purpose for procreation, that His kingdom be expanded (Exod. 3:6).

The Federal Theory

This theory states that Adam, as both the physical and federal head of the human race, brought sin and accompanying guilt to the entire race. It uses Adam's federal status as the basis for imputation of sin and death as its penalty.

This theory contradicts the teachings of the Bible, which states that all sinned in and with Adam. Another problem with this theory is that it does not acknowledge the parallelism between Adam and Jesus, a foundational truth in God's plan of redemption. Jesus was manifested in the fullness of time to redeem them who were under the law that they might receive the adoption of sons (Gal. 4:4–5; 1 Cor. 15:45).

The Theory of Corporate Personality

The theory of corporate personality states that an individual can act on the behalf of or represent a group of other individuals because of the close association or relationship they share. H. Wheeler Robinson promulgated this theory using a few examples from the Old Testament, in particular, the Lord's judgment of Korah, the son of Izhar, and of Dothan and Abiram, the sons of Eliab, to support his argument. Their entire families were condemned and destroyed with them consequent on their sins.

However, there are many problems with this view, and the Bible does not support this theory. To mention two, it does not acknowledge that all men participated in the sin of Adam and share the guilt accompanying that sin, nor does it acknowledge the important parallelism between Adam and Jesus Christ, through whom men are set free from the bondage of sin and Satan (1 Cor. 15:45; Rom. 5:14–18).

The Creation Theory

This theory states that God immediately creates the soul of every person born into the world, the soul entering the body at a very early stage of its development, perhaps at conception. Like the preexistence theory, this theory was promulgated by an early philosopher who has not been identified. We know it is an early thinker, for Aristotle, Ambrose, Jerome, and Pelagius subscribed to this theory; other philosophers, Anselm and Aquinas, and most of the Roman Catholic and Reformed theologians also support this theory.

Many philosophers and theologians embrace this theory because it bears a surface resemblance to the biblical account and explains why Jesus did not inherit the sinful nature of his mother. But a careful analysis reveals several distinctive differences between this theory and the biblical or Traducian account. The creation theory teaches the following:

1. The body alone propagates from previous generations.

2. God is present in essence in all flesh.

3. God himself directly creates the soul and spirit of every person separate and distinct from the body.

4. God unites the soul, the spirit, and the body of the child at the point of conception in the womb or immediately thereafter.

However, the Bible contradicts these positions; creationism cannot account for the fact that children bear resemblance of their parents and grandparents, sometimes as far as the fourth generation. Genesis 1 states that God, in the process of creation of man, gave him the ability to reproduce after his kind. He placed the seed of His creation within them, equipping them to procreate after their own kind. The body and soul of mankind bears the image and likeness of their parents. "The heavens declare the glory of God and the firmament His handywork" (Ps. 19:1). Surely, there is evidence of God's presence in all the natural generation, but this is His mediate presence and not His essence.

CHAPTER 12

MAN'S STEWARDSHIP OF THE EARTH

The *Wiktionary* defines a steward as someone who supervises or manages property or affairs for another person or entity. *Wikipedia* defines stewardship as an ethical value that embodies the responsible planning and management of resources. The concept of stewardship in scripture refers to the use of all the resources God has provided mankind, material and spiritual, for His glory and the advancement of mankind. After working for five and a half days, God assigned Adam the task of managing everything He created (Gen. 1:28; Ps. 24:1). The universe was created with perfect balance, but that was somewhat eroded by Adam's sin and the consequent judgment God inflicted upon creation (Gen. 3:17–18; Rom. 8:21–22). God provided the criteria He employs regarding man's stewardship in conveying to Noah the decision He made to judge the earth by the flood. "The wickedness of man was great in the earth, and that every imagination of the thoughts of his heart was only evil continually" (Gen. 6:5).

The Lord exhibited His care for man throughout the scriptures. He heard the cries of Hagar, Abraham's concubine, and their son in the wilderness of Beersheba and provided their needs, promising to make Ishmael a great nation. In Matthew, Jesus said, "Behold the fowls of the air, for they sow not, neither do they reap, nor gather into barns; yet your heavenly Father feed them… Wherefore if God so clothe the grass of the field, which today is and tomorrow is cast into the oven, shall He not much more clothe you, O ye of little faith" (Matt. 6:26, 30).

Evidenced in Scriptures

"You shall not pollute the land where you are; for blood defiles the land; and the land cannot be cleansed of the blood that is shed therein, but by the blood of him that shed it. Defile not therefore the land which you shall inhabit, wherein I dwell; for I the Lord dwell among the children of Israel" (Numbers 35:33–34). The Lord in this text was addressing the establishment of cities of refuge for persons who may have accidently killed someone and were seeking a place of safety from family members of the victim, who may wish to seek revenge for their loss. Although the application here is indirect, the principle of diligent stewardship is evident, not only of the land, but of the lives of the families involved and the community at large.

The children of Israel were commanded to keep the Sabbath, a time of rest from their labor and a time to worship the Lord on the seventh day of each week (Exod. 20:8–11). The land also in the ancient Jewish economy was given a Sabbath, a time of rest, every seventh year.

> Six years thou shall sow thy field and six years thou shall prune thy vineyard and gather in the fruit thereof. But in the seventh year shall be a sabbath of rest unto the land, a sabbath for the Lord, thou shalt neither sow thy field, nor prune thy vineyard. That which growth of its own accord of thy harvest, thou shalt not reap, neither gather the grapes of thy vine undressed: for it is a year of rest unto the land. (Lev. 25:3–5)

The ancient Jewish economy also included the year of Jubilee, a time of Sabbath rest, homecoming, liberation, and restoration for the people (Lev. 25:8–18).

> Just as the people were to come up to the mountain at the sounding of the … shofar to commemorate its union with the Lord, so at the expiration of the seventh sabbatical year, the trumpet blast was to announce to the covenant nation the gracious presence of its God, and the coming of the year

which was to bring liberty throughout the land to all that dwelt therein: deliverance from bondage; return to their property and family; and release from the bitter labor of cultivating the land. This year of grace was proclaimed and began with the Day of Atonement of evert seventh sabbatical year, to show that it was only with the full forgiveness of sins, that the blessed liberty of the children of God could possibly commence.[37]

The statutes God instructed His people, the nation of Israel, to observe clearly and reveal the quality of stewardship He requires of mankind. The Lord chose Israel as a model nation, through whom He will bless all the nations of the world, and sealed this plan by the covenants He made with their forefathers, Abraham, Isaac, and Jacob (Gen. 22:17–18; Exod. 19:5–6). Hence, these statutes established the level of stewardship God requires of mankind. The author will use an extract from Ralph F. Wilson's series on the book of Isaiah.

You have not looked unto the maker thereof, neither had respect unto him that fashioned it long ago, Isaiah 22:11b. They have trusted in their own works, rather than the grace of God, and so have committed the unforgiveable sin of unbelief, Isaiah 22:14. Now Isaiah turns to two individuals who are officers in Hezekiah's administration, Shebna, Hezekiah's secretary is referred to as this steward... This self-important man is preparing a fine tomb for himself on the heights of the city while Jerusalem itself is threatened. He is expendable (Verses 15–19). Perhaps this is an example of corruption, using the nation's resources to further one's own purposes and pride. Whatever Shebna's exact sins, God is angry with his stewardship. Shebna will be replaced by another steward, says Isaiah, Eliakim son of Hilkiah, who will be responsible

---

37   C. F. Keil and F. Delitzsch, *Biblical Commentary on the Old Testament*, 458.

for the security of the palace of the descendants of David[38]

God revealed His displeasure with the stewardship of many kings, priests, and other officials in both the Old and New Testaments. Another example from the Old Testament is recorded in Daniel.

> And thou his son, O Belshazzar, hast not humbled thine heart though thou knew all this. But hast lifted up thyself against the Lord of heaven; and they have brought the vessels of his house before thee, and thou and thy lords, thy wives and thy concubines, have drunk wine in them; and thou hast praised the gods of silver and gold of brass, iron, wood, and stone; which see not nor hear, nor know, and the God in whose hand thy breath is and whose are all thy ways, hast thou not glorified. Then was the part of the hand sent from Him; and this writing was written. MENE, MENE, TEKEL U-PHAR'SIN, this is the interpretation, God hath numbered thy kingdom, and finished it.
>
> Thou art weighted in the balances and art found wanted. Thy kingdom is divided and given to the Medes and Persians. (Dan. 5:22–28)

Belshazzar, the king of the Chaldeans, was slain the same night of the banquet, and Darius the Median took the kingdom and appointed Daniel, the prophet and man of God, as chief of the presidents of the kingdom. Daniel exhibited such a high standard of stewardship that he was retained as head of the princes and presidents by three kings, Nebuchadnezzar, his son Belshazzar, and Darius.

An example from the New Testament is recorded in the book of Acts. King Herod, seeking to please the Jews who despised the teaching of the apostles, killed James, the brother of John, and arrested Simon Peter. He commanded his soldiers to secure him in the innermost prison, where he was chained both hands and feet. It was during the

---

38   Ralph F. Wilson, jesuswalk.com/Isaiah/03_judgment.

days of unleavened bread in the Feast of Passover, and the king intended to present Peter to the people after the feast, but the Lord had another plan. He sent an angel to release Peter from prison.

> And when Herod had sought for him and found him not, he examined the keepers and commanded that they be put to death. And he went down to Caesarea and there, abode… And upon a set day Herod arrayed in royal apparel sat upon his throne and made an oration unto them. And the people gave a shout saying, it is the voice of a god, and not a man. And immediately, the angel of the Lord smote him, because he gave not God the glory; and he was eaten of worms and gave up the ghost. But the Word of God grew and multiplied. (Acts 12:19–24)

Evidenced in Modern Times

I will examine the collapse of the Soviet Union and the increasing global warming crisis in my discussion of stewardship in modern times. On January 1, 1991, the Soviet Union was the largest country in the world, covering some 8,650,000 square miles, nearly one-sixth of the earth's land mass. Its population numbered more than 290 million, and 100 nationalities lived within its borders.

Its colonies were Armenia, Azerbaijan, Belarus, Estonia, Georgia, Kazakhstan, Kyrgyzstan, Latvia, Lithuania, Moldova, Tajikistan, Turkmenistan, Ukraine, and Uzbekistan. The USSR boasted an arsenal of tens of thousands of nuclear weapons, and its sphere of influence, exerted through such mechanisms as the Warsaw Pact, extended throughout Eastern Europe. Yet within a year, the Soviet Union ceased to exist. While it is impossible to pinpoint a single cause for an event as complex and far-reaching as the dissolution of a global superpower, several internal and external factors were certainly at play in the collapse of the USSR.[39]

---

39   Michael Ray, Britannica.com, Soviet Union Collapse.

Mikhail Gorbachev, who was appointed General Secretary of the Communist Party of the Soviet Union (CPSU) on March 11, 1985, set out to jump-start the national economy and to streamline the cumbersome government bureaucracy. When his initial attempts failed to yield results, he implemented the policies of glasnost, that is, openness to foster dialogue with the people and perestroika, restructuring to quasi-free market policies for government-run industries. The state lost control of the media and the public sphere, and democratic reform movements began to arise throughout the nation. Gorbachev's reforms and his abandonment of the Brezhnev Doctrine, whereby USSR intervened to strengthen its hold where its socialist rule was threatened, hastened the demise of the Soviet empire.

Economic factors[40] played a huge part in the collapse. Shortages of consumer goods were routine, and hoarding was commonplace. The Soviet black-market economy was estimated to be more than 10 percent of the nation's GDP. Wage hikes were supported by printing money, escalating inflation. Fiscal policy mismanagement made the nation vulnerable to external factors. The sharp drop in the price of oil from $180 to $24 a barrel in March 1986 sent the economy into a tailspin, the energy resources being the nation's main provider of foreign capital. Gorbachev was appointed president for a term of five years on March 14, 1990. The oil price spiked temporarily during the Iraq invasion in August 1990, but by that time, the Soviet collapse was well under way.

A committee of eight officials, led by Vice President Gennady Yanayev, representing the old political, economic, and social order, staged a coup at 6:00 a.m. on August 19, 1991. They placed President Gorbachev under house arrest and announced via Radio Moscow that his ill health necessitated the relinquishment of his duties, which was now Yanayev's responsibility. They immediately banned strikes and demonstrations and imposed press censorship. The signing of a new union treaty aimed at encouraging more dialogue was scheduled to take place the following day, hence the timing. The military moved tanks onto the streets of Moscow, but the population of the city immediately began to dissuade the troops from obeying the orders of

---

40   Ibid.

the committee who organized the coup, and began to set up barricades around the White House.[41] The president refused to cooperate with the committee and got the support of Boris Yeltsin, who was able to get into the Russian White House and rally support against the coup. At 12:50 p.m., Yeltsin, standing on a tank in front of the White House, publicly condemned the coup, calling the organizers criminals and traitors and called for a general strike. At Yeltsin's request, Aleksey II, patriarch of the Russian Orthodox Church, condemned the coup and criticized the detention of the president. Lieutenant General Viktor Samsonov placed the city of Leningrad under military control, announcing that he assumed the office of chairman of the city's emergency committee. Meanwhile, Leningrad's mayor, Anatoly Sobchak, returned from Moscow with the aid of loyal KGB agents and was able to persuade Chairman Samsonov and the troops to arrest the officers who organized the coup. President Gorbachev's bodyguards remained loyal and were able to set up a receiving set, permitting him to keep abreast of the developments via the BBC and *Voice of America* radio feed. While in Moscow, elite tank regiments defected and surrounded the White House in defense of the establishment. The coup failed for several reasons. Perhaps most important was Gorbachev's democratization initiative, which made public opinion very important, and officers and the population no longer stood silent accepting orders from above. The coup plotters were arrested while trying to leave the country. On August 21, 1991, the Soviet Supreme Court reinstated President Gorbachev and annulled all the decrees of the Emergency Committee.

Amid the chaos of the failed coup, Latvia, Lithuania, and Estonia declared their independence from the USSR on August 21, 1991. Ukraine, the largest Soviet Republic outside of Russia, declared its independence on August 24, 1991, and by the end of 1991, all the other Soviet republics, along with some subregions, including Chechnya, South Ossetia, Abkhazia, Transdniestria, and Nagorno-Karabakh, declared their independence from the USSR.[42] The demise of the USSR, however, gave rise to much growth and development of the individual independent states, which were, thereby, empowered to chart their own future and the social and economic welfare of their population.

---

41   Ibid.
42   Usrussiarelations.org, collapse of the Soviet Union.

I examined in detail the covenant God established with Noah, his sons, the earth, and every animal that entered the ark when I discussed the dispensation of human government in chapter 5. I now wish to refer briefly to that covenant as it relates to man's stewardship of the earth and God's creation therein.

> Behold I establish my covenant with you and with your seed after you, and with every living creature that is with you, of the fowl, of the cattle, and of every beast of the earth with you; from all that go out of the ark, to every beast of the earth. And I will establish my covenant with you; neither shall all flesh be cut off any more by the waters of a flood to destroy the earth. (Genesis 9:9–11)

The increasing crisis of global warming is a consequence of the lifestyle men have established on earth, much of which conflicts with the natural environment in which we live. New York City alone produces more than fourteen million tons of trash every year. Much of this waste is transported to landfills or incinerators; a small portion pollutes the streets and waterways. The mismanagement of waste is one of the many factors that contribute to global warming. Waste in the lakes, rivers, and oceans cause pollution, often resulting in the death of species of fish, other water population, and fauna. A warming climate can increase the risk of both underwater and aerial landslides, thereby increasing the risk of local tsunamis.

Other factors include consumerism, oil drilling, power-plant operations, the use of fossil fuels, emissions from motor vehicles, including farming equipment. These release greenhouse gases that damage the earth's ozone layer. Other harmful practices men engage in regularly is the use of chemical fertilizers in farming, overfishing, and industrialization, which necessitates cutting forests to build factories and establish new suburbs in the factory neighborhood. Effects arising from these practices include heat waves, longer droughts, wildfires, loss of flora and species of birds, ocean warming, flooding, raising of sea levels from melting glaciers, more intense tropical storms, and loss of ocean populations.

It is encouraging to see governments worldwide and the United Nations taking the issue of global warming seriously. Coalitions around the world are working to reduce carbon dioxide emissions, pursue nature-based solutions, extend sustainable energy initiatives, and invest in resilient cities, among other projects.[43]

Regarding the climate change crisis, a report published by a group of scientists led by James Hansen, a NASA climatologist, in April 2005 in the *Science* journal should dispel all doubts about forecasts on the issue. The five-year study employed more than two thousand monitoring stations around the world. They determined that temperatures would continue a slow rise, even if greenhouse gases are capped immediately, and will spin out of control if strong corrective action is not taken. Holland committed to cut emissions by 80 percent, the United Kingdom committed to cut them by 60 percent, Germany committed to cut them by 50 fifty, but the United States of America made no commitment, claiming they were facing an energy crisis. Overwhelming opinion polls revealed that American citizens support provisions that preserve air and water quality, control pollution, protect wildlife, and expand and preserve parklands. These firm convictions hold even when tax increases are required for funding.[44] America is, by far, the world's leading polluter, and the government's abandonment of its responsibilities is just another tragic step in a series of actions that have departed from the historic bipartisan protection of the global environment. The nation's proper stewardship of God's world is a personal, political, and moral commitment.

---

43   Un.org, climate change.
44   Jimmy Carter, *Our Endangered Values,* 173, 176–177.

CHAPTER 13

THE RAPTURE OF THE BODY OF CHRIST

The rapture is that glorious mystical event whereby the dead or, rather, the sleeping believers in Christ will be transformed in an instant, clothed with their immortal bodies and be caught up into the clouds to meet Christ, who will take both groups to heaven to abide with Him forever (John 14:1–3; 1 Cor. 15:51–54; 1 Thess. 4:13–17). The Bible calls the rapture a mystery because this truth was not revealed in the Old Testament times. It was revealed to man during the ministry of Jesus and the apostles. One of the main texts on this truth states,

> Behold I shew you a mystery; we shall not all sleep, but we shall all be changed. In a moment, in the twinkling of an eye, at the last trump; for the trumpet shall sound, and the dead shall be raised incorruptible, and we shall be changed. (1 Cor. 15:51–52)

The phrase *caught up* means snatched up or taken away. The Greek preposition *ek*, interpreted, "from," is used in this text, as it is used in Revelation 3:10. It conveys the idea of a "separation from." Believers will be separated from the world and the wrath of God that will be outpoured upon those that dwell on the earth.[45] The scriptures also

---

45   Rhodes, *The End Times in Chronological Order*, 44.

call the rapture the blessed hope of the universal church; it connotes a joyful anticipation of the fulfillment of all the glorious promises of God to His people. Paul, writing to Titus, states, "Looking for that blessed hope and the glorious appearing of the great God and our Savior Jesus Christ" (Titus 2:13). John looking forward to that moment said that as sons of God, they now have an assurance of this glorious hope, which purifies the believer, for when Christ appears, all believers shall be like Him, for they shall see Him as He is (1 John 3:2–3). In their immortal bodies, the saints will no longer suffer lack, sickness, pain, or death. Theologians hold varying beliefs regarding the timing of the rapture of the church, the body of Christ. Most, including the writer, however, are of the belief that the scriptures affirm a pretribulation rapture. I will examine the various arguments for and against each view. There are three schools of thought on this subject among born-again scholars: pretribulation, midtribulation, and post tribulation rapture.

I am aware of the millennial school of thought, which is held by some congregational denominations. They believe that there is no future earthly millennium kingdom but believe that Jesus is now reigning spiritually over His kingdom, and the devil is bound in this the church age. Clearly, the description of the binding of Satan in the book of Revelation is complete; he is bound with chains, thrown into the bottomless pit, and sealed there for a thousand years. During that time, he makes no appearance, and the Lord punishes sin instantly, ruling the inhabitants of the earth with a rod of iron. The persons who hold these beliefs do not possess the Holy Spirit and, hence, cannot receive or understand the Word of God, for spiritual things are spiritually discerned (Rev. 20:1–3; 1 Cor. 2:14). No born-again believer holds the aforementioned beliefs.

The midtribulation argument contends that the rapture of the church will take place at the middle of the seven-year period of tribulation and prior to the commencement of the Great Tribulation. This argument is supported by Gleason Archer, Oliver Buswell, and Merrill C. Tenney. These persons believe that God will purge the church during the first three and a half years of the tribulation and rapture the purified church to heaven before outpouring His wrath upon the earth. They claim that the last trumpet in the book of

Revelation sounds at the middle of the tribulation period and that the two witnesses represent the church. Scriptures they use to support their argument may include 1 Peter 4:12, 17–19, and Revelations 7:14–15. The teachings of the scriptures, however, do not support these views. First, the Lord promised to keep the church from the time of testing, also referred to as Jacob's Trouble (Rev. 3:10), and second, the body of Christ is not destined to experience the wrath of God but His salvation (1 Thess. 1:10; 5:9).

The post-tribulation argument, which is supported by Eldon Ladd and Robert Gundry, among other theologians, contends that the rapture of the church will take place after the Great Tribulation. Their concept is that the church will be cleansed and preserved during the tribulation and raptured prior to the battle of Armageddon, when Christ will appear in the clouds. They do not see the church going to heaven at the rapture but being transformed in the skies and returning to reign with Him in the millennium kingdom after the battle of Armageddon. They misinterpret Revelation 20:4 as referring to the church, not distinguishing the church from the tribulation saints to whom that text refers.

The scriptures, however, do not support this concept for many reasons. First, the scriptures state that Christ will return secretly in the clouds for His church before the tribulation and to the earth after the Great Tribulation to defeat the armies gathered to destroy Jerusalem and establish His millennium kingdom. Second, the Lord promised to keep the church from the hour of testing "because thou hast kept the word of my patience, I also will keep thee from the hour of temptation, which shall come upon all the world" (Rev. 3:10). The tribulation will test not some but all the world; hence, the church cannot be in the world at that time. Third, after the rapture, the church must go to heaven to participate in the bema seat judgment to be purified and rewarded for their works and, thereafter, in the great marriage feast of the Lamb (2 Cor. 5:10; Rev. 19:5–9).

The pretribulation argument states that Christ will secretly appear in the clouds to rapture His church at the end of the church age and prior to the beginning of the seven-year tribulation period. Noteworthy is the pattern set in the Old Testament with God's judgments of Sodom and Gomorrah, the nation of Egypt. He rescued Lot and his family from Sodom and Gomorrah and protected the land of Goshen, where the children of Israel dwelled during the plagues that inflicted the nation of Egypt, and the Lord rescued Rahab (who rescued the Jewish spies) and her family before judging Jericho (Gen. 18:23–24; Exod. 8:22–24; Josh. 6:25).

This concept recognizes the distinction God has made between the church and the nation of Israel. The Lord paused His prophetic program with the nation of Israel after they rejected and crucified their Messiah, and grafted the Gentile nations into His kingdom together with those Jews who accepted the gospel of Christ (Rom. 11:25; 31–32). After the rapture of the church, God will resume His covenant dealings with the nation of Israel. When the purpose of the tribulation is examined, the reader will recognize that its target excludes the church, whom Christ has destined for redemption and salvation. The tribulation is termed the hour of testing for the inhabitants of the earth and the outpouring of the wrath of God on the ungodly. The scriptures indicate that the culmination of the church age coincides with the "coming in of the fullness of the Gentiles" (Rom. 11:25). Accordingly, the scriptures fully support the pretribulation argument, which I endorse.

Church: Wheat and Tears

The church is a legal social organization where all are welcome to gather and seek the counsel of God and the support of the people of God in meeting their daily spiritual and material needs, where possible. The church, however, is not a product of man's imagination but of God and is much more than a social organization. In the concept of the scriptures, the church is the body of Christ Jesus and is a living vibrant organism that was birthed on the day of Pentecost in the city of Jerusalem (John 1:12–13; Acts 2:1–8). Throughout the generations of mankind, people have been seeking to establish themselves in life by seeking the guidance of God. The True and Living God provided much evidence in nature of His presence, wisdom, and power and completed the revelation of Himself and His divine purposes via the holy scriptures. The corrupt nature of man has led many to misinterpret the scriptures and establish churches with dogmas that violate the counsel of God. Because of this fact, there are entire denominations that deny the orthodox teachings of the Bible. Consequently, every congregation does not embrace the orthodox doctrines of the Bible (Isa. 55:8–9).

Jesus taught many times using parables to illustrate his lesson. He shared a parable about the kingdom of God likened unto a farmer who sowed good seeds of wheat in his field and went home, but while he slept, an enemy sowed tare in his field. When the wheat began to sprout, the tares also began to shoot up. The servants were tempted to promptly extract the tares but were advised by the wise owner to permit them to grow together until the day of harvest, lest they uproot the wheat with the tares. The lesson is, as it is in the natural, so it is in the spiritual realm. Pastors and teachers are required to diligently care for their congregants within reasonable boundaries, regardless of their response to their teachings (1 Tim. 2:15–26; 2 Tim. 4:1–5).

In His dialogue with Nicodemus, Jesus said that a person cannot perceive the kingdom of God except they are born of the Holy Spirit. The born-again believers are those persons who have surrendered their lives to the lordship of Jesus Christ; they are the persons who have been delivered from the kingdom of darkness and have been translated into the kingdom of God (Col. 1:13; John 1:12–13). Every congregation will constitute a percentage of persons who have not had that experience; they represent the tares in the parable, while the born-again believers represent the wheat (John 3:1–7).

True Church: The Body of Christ

The term *church* is used in two senses, the universal or worldwide and intergenerational church and the local church. The church is not the building in which the saints meet but the collective body of believers whom God has separated from the world unto Himself and empowered to live holy lives among a perverse generation. These people, like the disciples of old, have been given the gift of the person of the Holy Spirit, who draws them into a growing relationship with the Lord Jesus Christ. Being baptized into the body of Christ, the believers have become new creatures, sharing the very nature of the True and Living God (Rom. 6:1–6; 2 Cor. 5:17). Christ said, "I will build my church and the gates of hell shall not prevail against it" (Matt. 16:18b). He conveyed that, first, the church was not to be a continuation of the old economy that existed in the Old Testament and, second, it was not yet in existence.

The church, the body of Christ, is separate and distinct from the nation of Israel and from the Gentile nations for several reasons the writer will seek to outline here.[46]

1.   It comprises both Jews and Gentiles, persons who have been born of the Holy Spirit and baptized into the body of Christ by faith in Christ (Gal. 2:16).

2.   It is described as "one new man." Israel is a nation by natural birth while the church is a new man by new birth; that is regeneration by the Holy Spirit (Eph. 2:15).

3.   Every person in the church receives the same designation— believer, saint, or Christian—while no Gentile who joins himself to Israel is called an Israelite (Gal. 3:27–28).

4.   The church in scripture is referred to as the betrothed, yet to be married to Christ, while Israel is referred to as the married, then divorced, and yet to be remarried to Christ their Messiah (Matt. 22:1–14; Jer. 3:1, 20; Ezek. 16:15).

5.   All believers in Christ who died will be resurrected in the rapture to be with the Lord, but the Old Testament saints, Jews and Gentiles, will be resurrected after the great tribulation (1 Cor. 15:51–57; Isa. 26:19; Dan. 12:2).

Apostle Paul, in addressing the administration of spiritual gifts, affirms that the body of Christ constitutes many members equipped skillfully by the Holy Spirit to execute the purposes of God in the earth. Like the human body constitutes many members that are united and submitted to the head, so the body of Christ is submitted to the Headship of Christ (Eph. 1:22; 1 Cor. 12:12–27). The body of Christ constitutes Jews and Gentiles, people from every generation, race, country, culture, language, and economic and intellectual level. Like the human body, the church exhibits a distinctive structure, led by the

---

46   Norman Manzon, biblestudyproject.org.

fivefold giftings. Apostle Paul, to whom the Lord gave the marvelous revelation of the New Covenant embodying the dispensation of grace, recorded,

> He that descended is the same that ascended, far above all heavens, that he might fill all things. And He gave some apostles, and some prophets, and some evangelists, and some pastors and teachers, for the perfecting of the saints, for the work of the ministry, for the edifying of the body of Christ. Till we all come in the unity of the faith, and of the knowledge of the Son of God, unto a perfect man, unto the measure of the stature of the fullness of Christ. (Eph. 4:10–13)

There are several very important truths expressed in this text. First, each member of the body of Christ has a specific role or function to perform to edify and mature the saints for the glory of God and is required to work in conjunction with the other members to accomplish this purpose. Second, the teachings of the fivefold ministry are required to be rounded and targeted to accomplish the unity of the faith and a full or growing knowledge of Jesus, the Son of God. Finally, the entire body of believers is required to consistently strive for perfection in their walk of faith as disciples of Christ (2 Tim. 2:15).

Nature of the Rapture

The Old and New Testaments consistently speak of bodily resurrections: the widow's son (1 Kings 17:21), the Shunammite's son (2 Kings 4:32–36), and the man who was revived by Elijah's bones (2 Kings 13:21). The bodily resurrection of the dead was certainly taught and believed from that time onward. I endorse the views of Henry C. Thiessen, who believed this concept was first evident in scriptures when Abraham told his servants that he and his son Isaac will return after their worship and sacrifice[47] (Gen. 22:5). Abraham had every intention of obeying God's command to offer his son on Mount Moriah but also trusted that God had a plan to resurrect him from the dead.

---

47   Thiessen, *Lectures in Systematic Theology,* 382.

The New Testament mentions five instances of bodily resurrections: Jairus's daughter (Matt. 9:24), the son of the widow of Nain (Luke 7:4), Lazarus (John 11:43), Dorcas (Acts 9:40), and Eutychus (Acts 20:9–12). Additionally, one of the writer's favorite texts records the resurrection of many saints shortly after the resurrection of Christ Himself from the dead (Matt. 27:52), the guarantee of every believer's future resurrection. Jesus and all the apostles taught about the bodily resurrection of both the saved and unsaved.

The scriptures refer to three types of resurrections: a spiritual resurrection, which takes place at conversion and is synonymous with regeneration (John 5:25); judicial resurrection, whereby the believer, by personal identification with Christ, is raised from the dead with Christ (Rom. 6:4; Eph. 6:5; Col. 2:12); and a physical resurrection (John 5:28).[48] Apostle Paul records that there is a natural body and a spiritual body (1 Cor. 15:44). The natural body comprises flesh and blood and is designed for dwelling on the earth, while the spiritual body comprises flesh and bones and is designed for heavenly dwelling. Continuing, Paul stated, "But now is Christ risen from the dead and become the first fruits of them that slept. For since by man come death, by man also come the resurrection of the dead" (1 Cor. 15:20–21). Christ was raised a physical body of flesh and bones and invited His disciples to handle Him to confirm that it was really Him and not a spirit (Luke 24:39). John writes, "It does not appear what we shall be, but we know that when He shall appear we shall be like Him; for we shall see Him as He is" (1 John 3:2b).

As the Lord ascended into the clouds and up to His Father in heaven, angels appeared announcing to the disciples that "this same Jesus, which is taken up from you into heaven, shall so come in like manner, as ye have seen Him go into heaven" (Acts 1:11b). Expounding the glorious hope of the believer in Christ, Paul records,

> We shall not all sleep, but we shall all be changed. In a moment, in the twinkling of an eye, at the last trump; for the trumpet shall sound, and the dead shall be raised incorruptible, and we shall be changed. For this corruptible must put

---

48   Ibid., 383.

on incorruption, and this mortal must put on immortality. (1 Cor. 15:51–53)

A parallel version of the rapture states,

> We which are alive and remain unto the coming of the Lord shall not prevent them which are asleep. For the Lord Himself shall descend from heaven with a shout, with the voice of the archangel, and with the trump of God: and the dead in Christ shall rise first. Then we which are alive and remain shall be caught up together with them in the clouds, to meet the Lord in the air, and so shall we ever be with the Lord. (1 Thess. 4:15–17)

One of the outstanding natures of the rapture of the church is the fact that it will occur suddenly, without notice. As a thief in the night, watch, therefore, for you know not the hour your Lord comes (Matt. 24:42; 1 Thess. 5:2). The scriptures have already established that the bodies of the believers in Christ will be like that of Jesus after His resurrection, so I wish to enumerate the list of evidence supporting the characteristics of Christ's body.

1. It comprised flesh and bones (Luke 24:39).

2. It retained the scars in His hands, feet, and side from the crucifixion (John 20:27).

3. The disciples physically handled him (Matt. 28:9; John 20:27–28).

4. It was visible (Matt. 28:17).

5. Jesus ate food (Luke 24:30; 42–43; John 21:12–13).

The Earth after the Rapture

I wish to provide a glimpse of the general atmosphere on the earth after the body of Christ and the tangible presence and power of the Holy Spirit have been removed. Addressing the event of the rapture, Jesus said, "Then shall two be in the field, the one shall be taken and the other left. Two women shall be grinding at the mill; the one shall be taken and the other left" (Matt. 24:40–41). This text addresses two impacts, the economic or labor market impact and the social and domestic impact. The world would lose very many of its most dependable and skilled workers at every level in governments, industries, educational institutions, and judicial, medical, military, and paramilitary agencies, among others.

As it relates to transportation agencies, including the airline industry, pilots will disappear, causing the aircrafts to crash, killing everyone on board. Motor vehicle drivers will disappear, causing crashes on every highway and roadway. Railway operators will be missing from their locomotives, causing train crashes. The world will be a humongous crash scene, total chaos, mass death, and destruction worldwide. Many parents, guardians, and heads of households will be missing, multiplying the disorganization of the society and nations overall. It will take much time for nations to come to grips with the situation. The scriptures indicate that the devil desires to kill, steal, and destroy, so this is the climate he relishes and will seize every opportunity to impede efforts to restore order (John 10:10).

Writing about the work of the Antichrist, Apostle Paul said, "For the mystery of iniquity doth already work; only he who now let will let until he be taken out of the way" (2 Thess. 2:7). I am confident that this text refers to the person of the Holy Spirit, who alone fits the requirement to impede the devil. Theodore Beza, a French Protestant theologian, supports this view. John states, "He who is in you is greater than he who is in the world" (1 John 4:4). The Greek word *anachaitizo*, translated, "restrain," carries the idea "to hold back from action, to keep under control, to deprive of physical liberty, as by shackling." This is what the Holy Spirit does in hindering the work of the devil and his agent, the Antichrist, in this the church age.[49] The work God has assigned the Holy Spirit in the church age requires His dominance of the work of the kingdom of darkness in the earth, particularly with regard to the race of man (Gen. 6:3).

---

49   Rhodes, *The End Times in Chronological Order*, 59.

I wish to record a few of the numerous scripture texts that affirm the active presence and omnipotent power of the Holy Spirit in the earth, via the body of Christ.

1. Blessed be the God and Father of our Lord Jesus Christ, who hath blessed us with all spiritual blessings in heavenly places in Christ. (Eph. 1:3)

2. For John truly baptized with water but ye shall be baptized with the Holy Ghost, not many days hence. (Acts 1:5)

3. For by one Spirit, we are all baptized into one body, whether we be Jews or Gentiles, whether we be bond or free, and have been all made to drink into one Spirit. (1 Cor. 12:13)

4. Know you not that you are the temple of God, and that the Spirit of God dwelleth in you. (1 Cor. 3:16)

5. He that keeps His commandments dwells in Him, and He in him. And hereby we know that He abides in us, by the Spirit which He hath given us. (1 John 3:24)

The tares—that is, the regular church members that were left behind after the rapture—will be tormented with regret for their carnal lifestyle and seek repentance. The 144,000 Jews empowered by the Holy Spirit to propagate the gospel of Christ to the nations of the world will seek to evangelize by various means of communication, perhaps as available today in the church age, in person, via radio, television, printed materials, Internet, and other media. The writings of King David indicate that the Holy Spirit will respond to those of "a broken heart and a contrite spirit" (Ps. 34:18; 51:17). However, the dominance of the kingdom of darkness on the earth will require believers to resist the forces of darkness by refusing to take the mark of the beast and refusing to renounce the name and worship of the True and Living God to the point of death. The Beast will enact laws making it impossible for anyone to legally engage in any business without the mark of the beast (Rev. 13:15–18).

A one-world government will be established, and martial law will be enacted, whereby the military enforcers will put to death anyone who refuses to take the mark and worship the Beast; millions of believers will be martyred worldwide if they fail to renounce the worship of Christ Jesus (Rev. 6:9–11). The invasion of privacy will be the order of the day, as every movement of individuals will be observed via public cameras, personal cell phones, iPads, tablets, and other multimedia gadgets. The justice system will not come to the mercy of believers as the forces of darkness will be in total control of every arm of the government. Even the religious bodies of that day will be agents of the Beast.

The Word of God is true that now is the acceptable time. Truly, now is the day of salvation, now in the dispensation of grace, for a time is coming when it will be extremely difficult to overcome the destructive demonic forces of darkness, and the few that do overcome will only do so by dying for the cause of Christ (Isa. 61:2; 2 Cor. 6:2; Rev. 6:9–11). The parallel in scripture will be the choice of Esau, who despised his birthright, estimating it worthless at that moment of temptation: "Lest, there be any fornicator, or profane person, as Esau, who for one morsel of meat sold his birthright. For ye know how that afterward, when he would have inherited the blessing, he was rejected, for he found no place of repentance, though he sought it carefully with tears" (Heb. 12:16–17).

Too many people are not aware of the privileged times in which they live, disregarding the purpose of life and the danger of ignoring the invitation of salvation offered by the Lord in these perilous times. I consider the unsaved members of my family, my son, and grandsons, for whom I have been consistently praying, and experience the desperation exhibited by the rich man who begged for Lazarus to warn his brothers who were alive against rejecting the counsel of God that leads to salvation (Luke 16:27–31). Many people in society, especially those who habitually attend church, have experienced the promptings and pleadings of the Holy Spirit regarding their salvation but did not deem any urgency in such a decision. In other words, the devil did to them what he did to me, deceiving them into a state of complacency and procrastination.

People are not aware that conviction cannot be generated by their desire. It is the work of the Holy Spirit. Jesus said, "No man can come unto me except he is drawn by my Father" (John 6:44). The devil, who blinds the eyes of the unsaved to the promptings of the Holy Spirit, prompts them to waver and procrastinate when they are finally under conviction of the danger of eternal damnation. I fell victim to this destructive trap of Satan until the Lord, in His mercy, opened my understanding to the following text: "He that being often reproved hardened his neck shall suddenly be destroyed, and that without remedy" (Prov. 29:1). He accomplished His mission of redemption by providing me with a vision of myself falling into hell as His final act of conviction.

CHAPTER 14

IMMORTAL CHURCH IN HEAVEN

The raptured saints, the body of Christ at this time, will possess their immortal bodies, like unto the glorious body of the Lord Jesus Christ. Noteworthy is the fact that the three persons in the Godhead work in perfect harmony to accomplish the purposes of God the Father. The Holy Spirit, who flows from both God the Father and God the Son, plays an integral role in the preparation of the body of Christ for her marriage. A part of this preparation is the necessary cleansing and purification of sanctification Paul refers to repeatedly in his epistles (1 Thess. 4:3; Eph. 1:4–5; 1 Peter 1:15–16). The epistles continually exhort believers to judge themselves and walk worthy of the calling God has revealed to them in His word. The letters to the churches in the book of Revelation provide the holy requirement the Lord has set for His bride, the church. Only those believers who submit to the Lordship of Christ via the government of the Holy Spirit will overcome the schemes of the devil in the guise of the flesh, self, and the world system (1 Peter 5:6–10; 1 John 2:13–17; Rev. 3:15–21).

The Bema Judgment

Accordingly, the saints will be cleansed and purified in the instant of their rapture and be rewarded according to their works on the earth in the judgment seat of Christ in heaven (Rom. 14:8–10; 1 Cor. 3:11–

15; 9:24–27). Paul likened the church to a spiritual building where the believers are lively stones built upon the sure foundation of Christ Jesus (1 Peter 2:5) and laborers in the work of the ministry positioned to build the kingdom of God by executing the visions and programs inspired and empowered by the Holy Spirit (John 15:4–8). Jesus said He is the owner and builder of the church—"I will build my church." There may be much construction work taking place in ministry, but were they birthed by the Holy Spirit? Jesus said, "You can do nothing without me, for what is born of the flesh is flesh and what is born of the Spirit is spirit" (Matt. 16:18; John 15:5b; 3:6).

The scriptures are consistent in both the Old and New Testaments that everyone will be required to give an account unto God for the deeds they have committed in their life on the earth.

> Let us hear the conclusion of the whole matter; fear God and keep His commandments; for this is the whole duty of man. For God shall bring every work into judgment, with every secret thing, whether it be good or whether it be evil. (Eccl. 12:13–14)

> It is appointed men once to die, but after this the judgment. (Heb. 9:27)

Using the analogy of sports, Paul stated, "If a man also strives for masteries, yet is he not crowned, except he strives lawfully" (2 Tim. 2:5). In the popular international game of cricket, the umpire does not provide his final decision on an appeal for out until he verifies that the delivery by the bowler was a legal delivery—that is, he must first confirm that the bowler did not bowl a no-ball. For if the delivery was a no-ball, the batsman is deemed not out, even though the wicket was broken or the fielder took a clean catch or the wicket keeper removed the bails while the batsman was out of his crease. The scriptures established a scale into which all believers' works are classified; they are graded based on their combustibility. They are likened unto building materials, for the church is likened unto a lively building, Christ being both the chief cornerstone and the sure foundation (Matt. 21:42–44; Eph. 2:19–22). The materials range from straw, hay, cardboard, plastic, wood, stones, and various metals and are tried by fire.

Fire in the scriptures symbolizes the holiness of God, the Word of God being quick, sharp, powerful and a discerner of the thoughts and motives of man's heart (Heb. 12:29; 4:12). The judgment seat of Christ (bema seat) will be focused on the believer's personal stewardship of the gifts, talents, opportunities, and responsibilities provided him in life. This judgment by the Lord will not be a public process like the process in the court systems of nations today but will be a personal and private process between the Lord and the individual members of His bride, whereby their motives in ministry will be examined. They will receive rewards for their labor of love that glorified the Father, or they will be reprimanded for the opportunities they lost to glorify Him. The believers' works of hay, straw, cardboard, plastic, and wood would not survive the fire of God; these persons would suffer humiliation[50] (1 John 2:28).

The scriptures infer that the bema judgment will take place immediately after the rapture for two reasons. First, the twenty-four elders, whom scholars believe represent the church, cast their crowns before the throne of God in worship sometime after the rapture. Second, the bride of Christ is recorded as being adorned in fine linen, clean and white, representing the righteousness of saints, when they appear with Christ at His Second Coming, during the battle of Armageddon (Rev. 19:8).

The Marriage Feast of the Lamb

The Bible describes the relationship between Christ and the church as a marriage, Christ being the bridegroom and the universal church being the bride. Jesus Christ, the Lamb of God, often referred to Himself as a bridegroom (Matt. 9:15; 22:2–14; John 3:29). The three-phase process of the Hebrew marriage, which was referred to earlier, is the imagery employed by the scriptures. God the Father of the Bridegroom is also the Father of the bride because the individual members of the church were drawn to Christ by God the Father. Jesus said, "No man can come to me except the Father, which hath sent me draw him; and I will raise him up at the last day" (John 6:44). The Father, through His foreknowledge, predestinates, calls, and justifies

---

50   Ibid., 69.

the believers who accept His invitation of salvation by faith in Jesus Christ and baptizes them into the body of Christ (Rom. 8:28–30; 6:4). During this the church age, Christ the Bridegroom is preparing a place for His bride in His Father's house.

In the second phase of the marriage, the bridegroom comes to claim his bride and take her to the place prepared in his father's house. The church is portrayed as the virgin bride awaiting her heavenly Bridegroom. The Hebrew bride does not know the exact timing of her groom's arrival, so the church is exhorted to keep herself pure and unspotted from the world as she awaits the imminent return of her Groom (2 Cor. 11:2; Rev. 19:7–9). Christ the Bridegroom will come to claim His bride at the rapture and take her to heaven, where He is now preparing an abode in His Father's house. The marriage ceremony and the marriage feast will take place in heaven after the bema judgment.

Traditionally, the Hebrew marriage supper is convened days after the marriage feast and may last several days, depending on the resources and wishes of the bridegroom's father. I join the theologians who believe that the marriage supper of the Lamb will be convened in Jerusalem during the seventy-five-day interval between the end of the Great Tribulation and the commencement of the millennial kingdom. I also endorse the views of Ron Rhodes, who indicates that the judgment of the nations and the judgment of the twelve tribes of Israel will precede the convening of the great celebration of the marriage supper of the Lamb. That will be the perfect atmosphere for the introduction of the millennial kingdom, for traditionally, the relatives and friends of the bride and bridegroom are invited to the Hebrew marriage supper (Matt. 22:2–9).

CONCLUSION

In His self-disclosure from the book of Genesis, the Lord revealed to Moses His nature and character, the nature of man, His aspirations for their relationship, the identity of man's archenemy the Devil, his character and evil devices. He also provided in the other books of the Bible, the gospels and the epistles, more than enough information about the provisions He has made for mankind to attain the aspirations He set for them. Included are the internal and external boundaries man needs to observe and maintain to secure the protection and the rewards available in this earthly pilgrimage and eternity.

Amazon
Top reviews from the United States

George Hartwell
5 stars - A book with a purpose and acceptance of God.
Reviewed in the United States on April 4, 2025

The pacing of the book is well-balanced, with each chapter building upon the last, creating a sense of progression that keeps readers engaged. Robertson's clear and thoughtful prose invites contemplation, making the reader reflect on their own understanding of God's purposes and how they can align their lives with these intentions.

Armida Wagstaffe
5 stars - Our lives have divine purpose.
Reviewed in the United States on January 23, 2025

Robertson offers actionable insights that encourage readers to align their lives with the principles discussed in the book. Whether addressing issues of personal identity, relationships, or community involvement, he provides a roadmap for living in accordance with divine purpose.

Jenna Lee Dy
5 stars - A book with empowering message to its readers!
Reviewed in the United States on January 6, 2025

God's Eternal Purposes for Mankind is a compelling and insightful work that invites readers to reflect on their spiritual journeys and the greater narrative of humanity. This message is empowering and liberating, inviting individuals to embrace their unique contributions to the world.

Melissa Pearson
5 stars - A book of theological insight and practical application
Reviewed in the United States on January 28, 2025

James V. Robertson's God's Eternal Purposes for Mankind is a thought-provoking exploration of the divine intentions behind human existence. With a blend of theological insight and practical application, Robertson delves into the core questions of purpose, meaning, and the overarching narrative of humanity as seen through a biblical lens.

Anthony Villa
5 stars - Reflections to our journey within God's plan
Reviewed in the United States on September 26, 2024

One of the standout aspects of the book is its emphasis on the individual's role within the larger tapestry of God's plan. Robertson encourages readers to reflect on their personal journeys, urging them to recognize that each life is significant in the context of God's eternal purposes.

Keith Harolds
5 stars - Empowering Readers to Embrace Their Unique Contributions
Reviewed in the United States on March 13, 2025

The author's scholarly background is evident as he navigates complex theological concepts with clarity, making them accessible to readers regardless of their prior knowledge. This message is empowering and liberating, inviting individuals to embrace their unique contributions to the world.

Carl Anderson

5 stars - Insightful and Accessible Exploration of God's Eternal Purposes.
Reviewed in the United States on March 15, 2025

The book is structured in a manner that systematically unfolds the concept of God's eternal purposes, beginning with foundational theological principles and progressing toward practical applications in the lives of individuals and communities. Robertson's writing is scholarly and accessible, making complex theological ideas understandable to a broad audience, from lay readers to seasoned theologians.

Ace Garcia

5 stars - God's Eternal Purposes for Mankind is replete with practical applications!
Reviewed in the United States on February 21, 2025

The author's passion for the subject matter shines through, making it a worthwhile read for anyone seeking a deeper understanding of their place in God's grand design.

BIBLIOGRAPHY

Callahan, John. Neverthirst.org, bible/archives.

Carter, Jimmy. *Our Endangered Values*. New York.

Chambers, Oswald. *My Utmost for His Highest*. Grand Rapids, Michigan.

Evans, Tony. *Our God Is Awesome*. Chicago, Illinois.

Gallop, Roger G. *Evolution the Greatest Deception in Modern History*. Florida.

Graham, Ron. Simplybible.com.

Houdmann, Michael. Compellingtruth.org, seven-dispensations.

Jones, Timothy P. *Rose Book of Bible Charts, Maps and Timelines*. Peabody, MA.

Keathley, J. Hampton III. Bible.org, eternal state.

Keil, C. F. and Delitzsch, F. *Biblical Commentary on the Old Testament*. Edinburgh.

Manzon, Norman. Biblestudyproject.org.

McMahon, Matthew. Apuritansmind.com, creationism or Traducianism.

Nee, Watchman. *Secrets to Spiritual Power*. New Kensington, Pennsylvania.

Pink, Arthur. *The Divine Inspiration of the Bible*.

Ray, Michael. Britannica.com, Soviet Union collapse.

Rhodes, Ron. *The End Times in Chronological Order*. Eugene, Oregon.

Stedman, Ray. Raystedman.org, authentic Christianity.

Storms, Sam. Samstorms.org, mediate or immediate imputation.

Thiessen, Henry C. *Lectures in Systematic Theology*. Grand Rapids, Michigan.

Wilson, Ralph F. Jesuswalk.com, Isaiah/03-judgment.

ABOUT THE AUTHOR

James grew up in La Retraite Village, West Bank Demerara, Guyana, with his five siblings. His family became the custodians of the Christian Brethren Church in the village from 1956. He developed a genuine fear of God from a tender age and totally surrendered his life to Christ at the age of fourteen. He discovered real joy and fulfillment in working for the Lord and seized the opportunity to lead the youth ministry when he was just sixteen years of age. After marriage, he moved from the West Bank to live in the East Ruimveldt Housing Scheme, Greater Georgetown, and assumed fellowship with the Christian Brethren Church, Ebenezer Gospel Chapel under Pastor Melvyn F. Hunte. He was later ordained as the assistant pastor at that assembly and served there for twelve years until 1989 when he migrated to the United States of America with his family of five.

While in Guyana, he served in the Guyana Civil Service for eighteen years, holding several senior positions both in the civil and public sectors, including the Office of the President, State Planning Secretariat, Public and Police Service Commissions Secretariat, Guyana State Corporation, and the Demerara Woods Limited. However, his heartbeat was always the work of the ministry. He experienced real joy in worshipping the Lord and expounding the Word of God to others. The Lord led him to plant a church in the Mabura Community, Region 10, Guyana, in 1983 while he served as personnel manager and community development officer of the Demerara Woods Limited. While in Guyana, he earned an associate degree in public administration from the University of Guyana.

After migrating to the USA, he completed his bachelor's degree in business management and finance from Brooklyn College in 2000, a master's degree in theology in 2007, and a doctor of divinity degree in December 2022 from the Community Bible College and Seminary, Brooklyn, New York.

The Lord commissioned him to strengthen the arm of several Pastors in New York during his thirty-four years of residence in the USA. He has been involved in international ministry, conducting crusades and sharing at conferences in Guyana, St Vincent, and Central America, Panama and Costa Rica, in particular. He now serves in a small church with an international vision, the Rochdale Shepherd House Open Bible Church located in Queens, New York, USA.